Master Focus, Beat Procrastination, and Finish
What You Start—A Simple Time Management
System for ADHD Brains

THE

**ADHD
RESET TOOLS
FOR SHARPER
FOCUS AND
DAILY WINS**

5 MINUTE

F CUS

RESET

SCOTT ALLAN
FROM THE CREATOR OF DO THE HARD THINGS FIRST®

The 5-Minute **Focus** Reset

Scott Allan

Also By Scott Allan

NEVER GET STUCK AGAIN— DOWNLOAD THE ZERO PROCRASTINATION GUIDE AND TAKE CONTROL OF YOUR FUTURE TODAY!

Download the Zero Procrastination Guide

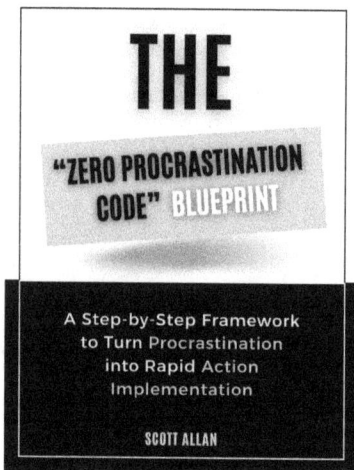

THE

"ZERO PROCRASTINATION CODE" BLUEPRINT

A Step-by-Step Framework to Turn Procrastination into Rapid Action Implementation

SCOTT ALLAN

scottallanbooks.com

The 5-Minute **Focus** Reset

MASTER FOCUS, BEAT PROCRASTINATION, AND FINISH WHAT YOU START—A SIMPLE TIME MANAGEMENT SYSTEM FOR ADHD BRAINS

Scott Allan

Scott Allan S A
B O O K S

Contents

For You—A Message from the Author

From Scott Allan

For most of my life, I struggled to focus.

I wasn't lazy. I wasn't unmotivated. I just couldn't seem to stay locked in on anything long enough to finish it—at least, not without a battle. I'd start strong, full of energy and ambition... and then drift. Or freeze. Or avoid. Or jump to something new.

It wasn't that I didn't want to follow through. I just couldn't seem to keep my attention steady long enough to *get to the end* of what I started.

If you've felt this way too—this book is for you.

It took me years to learn that I didn't need more pressure. I didn't need another productivity system, or a perfectly organized calendar, or the "right" routine.

What I really needed was a way to focus in small doses—something simple enough to do on a bad day, and strong enough to build real momentum on a good one.

The breakthrough came when I started thinking in **micro-tasks**.

Five minutes. One sentence. One small loop to close.

The more I practiced focusing small, the more I started finishing big.

And slowly, the chaos began to clear.

This book is the system I wish I had back then. It's not about perfection—it's about **returning**.

It's about learning to work *with* your brain, not against it.

And it's about building something you can come back to, no matter how many times you fall off.

I hope this book helps you feel less alone. I hope it gives you tools that actually work. And most of all, I hope it helps you finish the things that matter to you—on your own terms.

Here's to small steps.

And to the power of the next five minutes.

— *Scott Allan*

"That's been one of my mantras – focus and simplicity. Simple can be harder than complex: You have to work hard to get your thinking clean to make it simple."

—Steve Jobs

Introduction: You're Not Broken. You're Distracted.

For most of my life, I struggled to focus.

I wasn't lazy. I wasn't unmotivated. I just couldn't seem to stay locked in on anything long enough to finish it—at least, not without a battle. I'd start strong, full of energy and ambition... and then drift. Or freeze. Or avoid. Or jump to something new.

It wasn't that I didn't want to follow through. I just couldn't seem to keep my attention steady long enough to *get to the end* of what I started.

If you've felt this way too—this book is for you.

Why This Book Exists

I wrote this book because I got tired of being told to "just focus harder" or to "be more disciplined." I got tired of productivity systems designed for neurotypical brains that left me feeling more broken when I couldn't make them stick.

The world is full of focus advice that works perfectly—for brains that aren't wired like ours.

This book exists because I needed a different approach, and I'm guessing you do too.

It took me years to learn that I didn't need more pressure. I didn't need another productivity system, or a perfectly organized calendar, or the "right" routine.

What I really needed was a way to focus in small doses—something simple enough to do on a bad day, and strong enough to build real momentum on a good one.

The breakthrough came when I started thinking in **micro-resets**.

Five minutes. One intention. One small loop to close.

The more I practiced focusing small, the more I started finishing big.

And slowly, the chaos began to clear.

What Makes This Approach Different

Most productivity systems ask you to adapt to them. This book asks you to start where you are.

Most focus strategies are built on willpower and discipline. These resets are built on understanding how your brain actually works.

Most approaches shame you when you fall off track. This system expects imperfection and gives you a clear path back.

This isn't about transforming into someone with perfect focus. It's about becoming someone who knows how to return to what matters—again and again and again.

How to Use This Book

You don't need to read this book from cover to cover (though you certainly can). It's designed to work with the natural tendencies of ADHD brains:

If you're in crisis mode right now, flip to Chapter 13 for immediate emergency resets that can break the overwhelm cycle.

If you struggle with specific focus challenges, use the table of contents to find the reset that addresses your most pressing need:

- Morning overwhelm? Chapter 9
- Work distractions? Chapter 10
- Creative blocks? Chapter 11
- Evening wind-down? Chapter 12
- Clutter and environment? Chapter 7

If you want the complete system, start with Chapter 1 to understand the science behind your focus challenges, then work through each reset, implementing them one at a time.

Each chapter ends with a simple Action Step that you can implement in five minutes or less. These aren't just exercises—they're the building blocks of a focus system designed specifically for your brain.

What You'll Gain

This book won't give you superhuman focus or a perfect productivity record. What it will give you is:

- A set of practical, 5-minute reset techniques for different focus challenges

- A deeper understanding of how your brain actually works
- Freedom from the shame cycle of trying and "failing" at focus
- The ability to recover quickly when you inevitably get distracted
- A sustainable approach to finishing what matters to you

Most importantly, it will give you the confidence that comes from knowing you're not broken. Your brain is wired differently, and now you'll have tools designed specifically for that wiring.

A Note on Implementation

As you work through these techniques, remember:

1. **Start small**. Choose one reset that addresses your most pressing challenge and practice it consistently before adding others.
2. **Expect imperfection**. There will be days when you forget to reset or when nothing seems to work. This isn't failure—it's just part of having an ADHD brain in a distracting world.
3. **Value recovery over prevention**. The goal isn't to never get distracted. It's to

get better at noticing distraction and returning to intention without shame.

4. **Be patient with yourself**. You're learning a new relationship with your attention. That takes time.

Your First Reset Starts Now

Right now, as you're reading this, I want you to try something. Don't worry—it's not complicated.

Take a moment and notice: Where is your attention right now? Are you fully here with these words, or is part of your mind already thinking about what you need to do next?

Whatever you notice, don't judge it. Just observe it with curiosity.

Now, take one conscious breath. Feel your feet on the floor. Notice the weight of the book in your hands. Come back to this moment, to these words, to this choice to engage with something that might help you.

That's a reset. Gentle, simple, and entirely doable.

That's also the foundation of everything we're going to build together in the chapters ahead.

You're not broken. You're not behind. You're not starting from zero.

You're starting from right here, right now, with a brain that's capable of amazing things when you give it the right tools and the right environment.

Let's build those tools together.

— *Scott Allan*

SECTION 1:

Section 1: Understanding Your Focus Challenges

Chapter 1: Your Attention Isn't Broken— It's Overstimulated

I used to think there was something fundamentally wrong with me.

I'd sit down to write with the best intentions. Coffee ready, notes organized, laptop open to a fresh document. And for about twelve minutes, I'd be on fire—words flowing, ideas connecting, that sweet spot where everything clicks.

Then my phone would buzz. Just a quick check. Oh, and I should probably respond to that email while I'm thinking about it. Actually, let me grab some water first.

And on the way back, I'd notice my bookshelf needed organizing. Then I'd remember I wanted to research that productivity app everyone's talking about.

Two hours later, I'd find myself watching YouTube videos about ancient Roman architecture, wondering how I got there and why I couldn't just *focus* like a normal person.

This isn't a motivation problem. It's not a character flaw. It's neurobiology.

The Neuroscience of ADHD Focus

At its core, ADHD (Attention-Deficit/Hyperactivity Disorder) involves differences in how your brain regulates attention, manages impulses, and processes reward.

While everyone's brain is unique, ADHD brains show some consistent patterns:

Lower baseline dopamine levels. Dopamine is the neurotransmitter that helps regulate attention, motivation, and that feeling of satisfaction when you complete something. With less dopamine available, your brain is constantly seeking stimulation to boost those levels.

Altered executive function. The executive system in your brain—primarily housed in the prefrontal cortex—manages your ability to plan, prioritize, organize, and regulate behavior. In ADHD, this system develops differently and functions less efficiently.

Differences in the reward network. The brain's reward system helps you evaluate which activities are worth your time and attention. In ADHD, this network tends to favor immediate, novel rewards over delayed gratification.

Irregular activation patterns. Brain scans show that people with ADHD often have different activation patterns across multiple brain networks, particularly those involved in attention, motivation, and emotional regulation.

These aren't theoretical differences—they're physiological realities that affect how you experience the world every day.

The ADHD Focus Paradox

One of the most misunderstood aspects of ADHD is the false belief that it means "no attention." What it actually means is "inconsistent attention regulation."

ADHD isn't the inability to focus—it's the inability to consistently control *what* you focus on and for how long.

Think of it this way: Most people have attention that works like a flashlight—they can point it where they want, dim it or brighten it as needed.

Your ADHD brain is more like a laser pointer in the hands of a hyperactive cat. When it hits the target, it's incredibly powerful and precise—that's hyperfocus, the ability to become so absorbed in something interesting that hours disappear. But most of the time, it's bouncing around the room, chasing shadows you can't even see.

This explains why you can play video games for six hours straight but struggle to read an important email for five minutes. It's not about interest alone—it's about how your brain processes the neurochemical rewards from different activities.

What's Really Happening When You "Lose Focus"

Let's break down what's actually happening in your brain during a typical focus drift:

1. **Initial engagement:** You start a task with clear intentions. Your prefrontal cortex is activated, and you're consciously directing your attention.
2. **Stimulation assessment:** Your brain quickly evaluates the neurochemical reward value of the task. Is it novel? Interesting? Challenging in the right way?

If yes, you might maintain focus. If not, your brain starts seeking alternatives.

3. **Competing stimuli:** Something in your environment (a notification, a thought, a sound) offers the potential for more immediate stimulation. Your brain's reward system perks up.

4. **Attentional shift:** With lower inhibitory control, your attention shifts to the new stimulus before your conscious mind has fully registered the decision to switch.

5. **Stimulation loop:** The new activity provides a small dopamine hit, reinforcing the behavior and making it harder to return to the original, potentially less stimulating task.

This isn't procrastination in the traditional sense. It's your brain's attempt to regulate its own neurochemistry in the most efficient way it knows how.

The Modern World Is ADHD Kryptonite

Here's the thing nobody talks about: the world has gotten exponentially more distracting in the last twenty years, but our brains haven't evolved to handle it.

Right now, as you're reading this, your brain is being pulled in dozens of directions:

- That notification that just buzzed on your phone
- The seven browser tabs you have open "just in case"
- The conversation happening in the next room
- The mental to-do list running in the background
- The anxiety about the thing you forgot to do yesterday
- The planning for what you need to do later

If you had a neurotypical brain, you might be able to filter most of that out. But with ADHD? All of that noise is competing for the same limited pool of attention resources.

The modern digital environment is literally engineered to exploit the exact vulnerabilities in your attention system:

- **Variable reward systems** in social media (like the unpredictable nature of what you'll find when you check notifications) are particularly effective at hijacking ADHD brains.

- **Endless content streams** remove natural stopping points that might otherwise give your brain a chance to reassess and redirect.
- **Notification systems** create false urgency that triggers your brain's emergency response system.
- **Algorithm-driven content** learns exactly what keeps your attention and serves more of it, creating powerful feedback loops.

It's like trying to have a conversation in a crowded restaurant where everyone else gets noise-canceling headphones, but you have to listen to every single conversation happening around you.

Why Willpower Is a Losing Strategy

I spent years trying to solve my focus problems with more discipline. More willpower. Better planners. Stricter schedules. Productivity apps that promised to "hack my brain."

All of that failed spectacularly. Here's why:

Willpower is finite. It's like a muscle that gets tired. You might be able to force yourself to focus for an hour or two through sheer determination, but eventually, that muscle gives out. And when it does, you don't just return to baseline—you often bounce back worse than before.

ADHD brains burn through willpower faster. Every time you resist a distraction, every time you force yourself to stay on task when your brain wants to wander, every time you fight your natural impulses—you're depleting a resource that's already in shorter supply than most people's.

You can't discipline your way out of neurobiology. Trying to solve ADHD focus issues with willpower alone is like trying to solve nearsightedness by squinting harder. It might work temporarily, but you're fighting against how your brain is literally wired to function.

This explains why so many productivity systems fail for people with ADHD. They're built on the assumption that with enough discipline and the right structure, anyone can maintain consistent focus. But that's simply not how ADHD brains work.

A New Understanding: From Judgment to Data

The breakthrough moment for me came on a Tuesday afternoon when I was supposed to be writing but instead found myself researching the history of paper clips.

I was about to launch into my usual self-attack routine when I caught myself and asked a different question: "What if this isn't a failure? What if this is just information?"

Instead of berating myself for being "distracted," I got curious about what had happened. I traced the path: I was writing about organization systems, which made me think about organizing papers, which led to wondering about paper clips, which sent me down a research rabbit hole.

The drift wasn't random. It wasn't a moral failing. It was my ADHD brain following a perfectly logical trail of associated ideas—it just wasn't the trail I wanted to be on at that moment.

That's when I realized: I didn't need more discipline. I needed better navigation tools.

Your Brain Can Reset

The most important thing to understand about ADHD attention is this: your focus isn't permanently broken—it's temporarily redirected. And if it can be redirected away from what matters, it can also be redirected back.

Every moment of lost focus is also a moment of opportunity. The same brain that got distracted can learn to reset itself—not through force, but through understanding and intentional practice.

That's what the rest of this book is about: learning to work with your brain's natural patterns rather than against them. Developing simple, 5-minute reset techniques that acknowledge how your attention actually works and give you reliable ways to bring it back when it wanders.

These resets aren't about becoming a different person. They're about becoming a more intentional version of who you already are. Someone who can catch themselves when they drift. Someone who can redirect their attention without shame. Someone who can work with their brain's natural patterns instead of fighting them.

Action Step

Your focus problems aren't character flaws—they're the result of an ADHD brain trying to function in an overstimulating world.

The next time your attention drifts, resist the urge to criticize yourself. Instead, get curious: What pulled your attention away? What was your brain seeking? How long did it take you to notice the drift?

Write down your observations without judgment. This isn't failure—it's data collection about how your unique brain works.

This awareness is the foundation for all the reset techniques we'll develop in the chapters ahead.

Chapter 2: The Multitasking Trap—Why Your Brain Can't Handle "Just One More Thing"

I used to wear multitasking like a badge of honor.

In my corporate days, I'd pride myself on juggling twelve different projects, answering emails during meetings, taking notes while half-listening to conference calls, and mentally planning my weekend while pretending to focus on quarterly reports.

I thought I was being efficient. Productive. The kind of person who Gets Things Done.

What I was actually doing was training my brain to never, ever focus on just one thing. And for an ADHD brain that already struggles with attention regulation? That was like pouring gasoline on a fire.

Here's what no one tells you about multitasking: **it's not actually multitasking. It's rapid task-switching. And every switch costs you time, energy, and focus you can't afford to lose.**

The Multitasking Myth

Your brain cannot do two cognitively demanding tasks at the same time. That's not an ADHD limitation—that's a human limitation. Neurotypical brains can't truly multitask either.

What feels like multitasking is actually your brain frantically switching back and forth between tasks, like a tennis ball being whacked across a net. And each time it switches, it pays what researchers call a "switching cost."

Here's what that looks like in practice:

1. You're writing an email to a client
2. A notification pops up
3. Your brain disengages from the email
4. It takes 2-3 seconds to load the context for the notification
5. You read and respond to the message
6. Your brain disengages from that task
7. It takes 10-25 seconds to reload where you were in the email

8. You've lost your train of thought and have to reread what you wrote
9. You spend another 30 seconds getting back into the flow

That "quick" check just cost you at least 45 seconds. And that's assuming you don't get distracted by three other things while you're switching back.

For ADHD brains, those switching costs are even higher because we:

- Take longer to reload context after an interruption
- Are more likely to get distracted during the switch itself
- Have a harder time remembering where we were when we return
- Experience more frustration and mental fatigue from the constant switching

---

My Multitasking Reality Check

The moment I realized how destructive my multitasking habit had become was during a writing session that should have been simple.

What I planned: Complete an 800-word blog post in 3 hours with a clear outline.

What actually happened:

- Wrote only 200 words in 3 hours
- Checked email 47 times (I counted later)
- Responded to 8 unrelated messages
- Googled three things unrelated to my article
- Answered two phone calls
- Reorganized my desktop "because it looked messy"
- Started research for a completely different project

I felt busy. I felt productive. But I had accomplished almost nothing on the one thing I'd actually sat down to do.

That's when it hit me: **multitasking wasn't making me more productive. It was making me feel more productive while actually getting less done.**

The ADHD Multitasking Amplifier Effect

Here's why multitasking is especially brutal for ADHD brains:

We're already overstimulated. The dopamine deficit we discussed in Chapter 1 means your brain is constantly scanning for something more interesting, more novel, more rewarding. Every open tab, every notification, every potential task is like a shiny object calling to your attention-seeking brain.

We have poor impulse control around interesting stimuli. When something catches your ADHD brain's attention, it's genuinely hard to resist. That notification doesn't just represent a message—it represents potential novelty, social connection, maybe even praise or recognition.

We lose more in the transition. ADHD brains have working memory challenges, which means we're more likely to completely lose our train of thought when we switch tasks.

We get stuck in switching loops. You check email, which reminds you to update your calendar, which makes you think about that meeting next week, which makes you want to prepare for it, which requires opening a different document, which has a link you want to check...

Before you know it, you've been "working" for two hours and have no idea what you actually accomplished.

Prisha's Task-Switching Breakthrough

Prisha, a marketing manager with ADHD, described her typical workday as "digital pinball." Within fifteen minutes of starting her most important work, she'd have opened multiple emails, started unrelated projects, messaged colleagues, and somehow ended up ordering office supplies.

The breaking point came when she missed an important client deadline—not because she didn't have time, but because she'd spent the entire week in a constant state of task-switching.

Prisha began experimenting with what she called "mono-tasking"—working on only one clearly defined task at a time, with all potential distractions removed. She started small: 20 minutes of single-tasking followed by a 5-minute "switching break" where she could check messages.

"The difference was shocking," she shared. "I discovered I could complete in one focused 45-minute session what used to take me an entire scattered day."

Within two months, Prisha had not only caught up on her backlog but received a promotion based on the quality and timeliness of her work.

The Myth of the ADHD Multitasking Advantage

I hear this a lot: "But people with ADHD are supposed to be good at multitasking! We're creative! We think outside the box!"

Here's the truth: **ADHD brains are good at making connections between disparate ideas. That's not the same thing as multitasking.**

Yes, your brain can hold multiple concepts simultaneously and find interesting relationships between them. That's a genuine strength. But that happens *within* a single focus session, not by jumping between completely different tasks.

When you're writing and your brain makes a connection to something you read last week, that's creative thinking. When you're writing and you stop to check email, then research vacuum cleaners, then scroll social media, that's just distraction.

The Real Cost of Constant Switching

Multitasking costs you more than you realize:

Time: Research shows it can take up to 25 minutes to fully refocus after an interruption.

Energy: Every task switch requires mental effort. By the end of a day full of switching, you're exhausted from all the transitions.

Quality: When you're constantly switching, you never get into what psychologists call "flow state"—that magical zone where your best thinking happens.

Confidence: Nothing undermines your sense of competence like working hard all day and having little to show for it.

Joy: The satisfaction of completing something, of seeing a project through from start to finish—multitasking steals all of that from you.

What Single-Tasking Actually Looks Like

When I first tried to work on just one thing at a time, it felt impossible. My brain kept reaching for other tasks like a phantom limb.

But here's what I discovered: **single-tasking isn't about perfect focus. It's about choosing one primary task and catching yourself when you drift.**

Real single-tasking for ADHD brains looks like this:

- You sit down to write an email
- Your brain suggests checking your calendar "just to see what's next"
- You notice that impulse and gently redirect: "I'm writing this email first"
- You write two sentences, then think about lunch
- You notice that too: "Email first, lunch after"
- You finish the email (even if it takes longer than expected)
- Then, and only then, you choose your next task

It's not about becoming a focus robot. It's about becoming someone who notices when they're switching and chooses whether to follow that impulse or stay with their current task.

The One-Tab Rule

Here's a simple experiment that changed my entire relationship with multitasking:

For one week, only keep one browser tab open at a time.

When you want to look something up, close the tab you're currently on first. When you want to check email, close whatever you're working on. When you're done with email, close it before opening your next task.

This single change will show you:

- How often you unconsciously switch between tasks
- How much mental energy you spend managing multiple open loops
- How much calmer your brain feels when it's not tracking seventeen different contexts
- How much faster you actually complete things when you're not jumping around

---

Breaking the Multitasking Habit

If you've been a chronic multitasker for years (like I was), retraining your brain takes patience. Here's how to start:

Identify your switching triggers. For me, it was notifications, boredom, and that moment when a task started feeling difficult. What makes you want to jump to something else?

Create switching friction. Turn off notifications. Put your phone in another room. Use website blockers. Make it slightly harder to switch, so you have a moment to choose instead of reacting automatically.

Set micro-sessions. Instead of trying to focus for hours, commit to 15-20 minutes on one task. When the timer goes off, you can switch if you want to. Often, you'll choose to keep going.

Practice the pause. When you feel the urge to switch, pause for just five seconds. Ask yourself: "Am I switching because I'm done with this task, or because my brain is seeking stimulation?"

Celebrate single-task completions. Every time you start and finish something without switching, acknowledge it. Your brain needs to learn that completion feels better than constant switching.

Action Step

Multitasking isn't a productivity superpower—it's a focus killer that's especially damaging to ADHD brains. Single-tasking isn't about perfect focus; it's about conscious choice.

Pick one task you need to complete today, close everything else—literally everything—

and set a timer for 20 minutes. See what it feels like to do just that one thing.

Notice when your brain wants to switch, but don't judge it. Just gently return to your chosen task.

Chapter 3: The Dopamine Drift—When Your Brain Checks Out Without Permission

There's a moment that happens to me almost every day. I'll be working on something important—writing, planning, responding to emails—and suddenly, I'm somewhere else entirely.

Not physically. Mentally.

One minute I'm focused and engaged. The next, I'm staring at my screen, thoughts completely blank, as if someone just hit the reset button on my brain. Or I "wake up" to find myself scrolling through social media, with no memory of picking up my phone or making the conscious decision to stop working.

I call this "the drift." And if you have an ADHD brain, you know exactly what I'm talking about.

The drift isn't a choice. It's not laziness. It's not a moral failing. It's your brain's natural response when the task at hand isn't providing enough stimulation to keep your attention engaged.

Understanding this drift—why it happens, how to catch it, and what to do when you're in it—is one of the most important skills you can develop as someone with ADHD.

What the Drift Actually Feels Like

Let me paint some pictures you'll probably recognize:

The Blank Stare: You're reading something important, but you realize you've been looking at the same paragraph for five minutes without absorbing a single word. Your eyes are moving, but nothing is going in.

The Unconscious Switch: You sit down to work on a project and somehow find yourself reorganizing your desktop, researching a random topic, or scrolling through your phone with no memory of how you got there.

The Mental Fog: Your brain feels like it's wrapped in cotton. You can see the tasks in front of you, you know what you need to do, but you can't seem to generate the mental energy to engage with any of it.

The Time Void: You sit down to do something that should take 30 minutes, and three hours later you've accomplished almost nothing, but you can't quite account for where the time went.

These experiences aren't failures of willpower—they're predictable patterns of how ADHD brains respond when they're not getting enough stimulation.

My Most Expensive Drift

Let me tell you about the drift that cost me thousands of dollars and taught me just how serious this issue could be.

I was working on a proposal for a potential client—a big contract that could have changed my business trajectory. The proposal was due in three days, and I had all the information I needed. It should have been straightforward.

But every time I sat down to work on it, I drifted. I'd open the document with good intentions, read the first paragraph, and then... nothing. My brain would just check out. I'd find myself researching completely unrelated topics, organizing files that didn't need organizing, or staring out the window.

I told myself I was "thinking about it" or "getting inspired." But really, I was stuck in a drift loop. The task felt overwhelming, my brain wasn't getting the stimulation it needed to stay engaged, so it kept wandering off to find something more immediately rewarding.

Three days passed. I submitted nothing. I lost the contract.

That's when I realized the drift wasn't just an inconvenience—it was actively sabotaging my life.

The Three Types of Drift

After years of observation, I've identified three primary types of drift that affect ADHD brains:

1. The Passive Drift: Your body stays in place, but your mind checks out. You're physically present—staring at your document, sitting in your meeting—but mentally, you're gone. Your brain has essentially gone into standby mode because it's not getting enough stimulation from the current task.

2. The Active Drift: Your attention actively jumps to something more stimulating—social media, interesting articles, reorganizing your desk. This isn't a conscious decision; it's your brain automatically seeking the dopamine hit it's not getting from your intended task.

3. The Productive Drift: You switch to something that feels more productive but isn't what you intended to do. You sit down to write a report but end up organizing your email inbox instead. It feels like work, but it's actually a form of productive procrastination.

Recognizing which type of drift you're experiencing helps you choose the right intervention to get back on track.

Valencia's Afternoon Scroll Spiral

Valencia, a graduate student with ADHD, tracked her typical afternoon drift pattern and discovered a consistent sequence:

1. She'd sit down to work on her dissertation after lunch
2. She'd read a few paragraphs to "get back into it"
3. She'd check her phone "just for a second"

4. Twenty minutes of scrolling would pass before she realized
5. When she finally put the phone down, she'd feel foggy and resistant
6. The cycle would repeat until evening

Valencia's breakthrough came when she started treating these drifts as data rather than failures. She kept a simple "drift diary," noting when her attention wandered and what her brain seemed to be seeking.

The patterns revealed that her drifts typically happened during conceptually difficult sections of writing. Her brain wasn't being lazy—it was seeking relief from cognitive strain.

With this understanding, Valencia developed a simple reset protocol: when she felt the urge to drift, she would name where she was stuck, take a deliberate 5-minute break, then return with a smaller, more concrete next step.

"It didn't stop me from drifting completely," she noted, "but it gave me a way to catch myself earlier and come back more efficiently."

Catching the Drift in Real Time

The key to managing drift isn't preventing it entirely—that's probably impossible with an ADHD brain. It's learning to notice when it's happening and gently redirecting yourself back to intention.

Here are the early warning signs to recognize:

Physical signs:

- Your posture changes (you slump, or your head tilts)
- Your breathing becomes shallow
- You start fidgeting or restless movement
- Your eyes lose focus or start darting around

Mental signs:

- You reread the same sentence multiple times
- You realize you've been thinking about something completely unrelated
- You feel a sudden urge to do "just one quick thing"
- Your internal monologue goes quiet

Emotional signs:

- You feel bored, anxious, or restless

- You start feeling resistant to your current task
- You experience a vague sense of "something's not right"
- You feel the pull of more interesting activities

The moment you notice any of these signs, you have a choice point. You can either let the drift continue, or you can use it as a reset opportunity.

My Drift Detection System

After years of unconscious drifting, I've developed a simple system to catch myself in the moment:

The 10-Minute Check-In: I set a gentle timer to go off every 10 minutes when I'm working on something that requires sustained focus. When it chimes, I ask myself: "Am I still doing what I intended to do?"

The Breath Anchor: Throughout the day, I try to take conscious breaths and notice: "Where is my attention right now?" This isn't self-criticism— it's just data collection.

The Physical Reset: When I notice I'm drifting, I stand up, stretch, or change my physical position.

This interrupts the drift pattern and gives me a moment to choose what to do next.

The Curiosity Question: Instead of judging myself for drifting, I get curious: "What is my brain seeking right now? Stimulation? Rest? A different type of challenge?"

These simple techniques have dramatically reduced the time I spend in unconscious drift, not by eliminating drift entirely, but by catching it much earlier.

Working with Your Drift Patterns

Once you start paying attention, you'll probably notice your drift has patterns. Maybe you drift more in the afternoon, or when you're working on certain types of tasks, or when you're in certain emotional states.

Instead of fighting these patterns, you can work with them:

Schedule drift-prone work for your peak focus times. If you always drift after lunch, don't try to do your most challenging work then.

Build stimulation into boring tasks. Play instrumental music, work in a coffee shop, use a standing desk, or gamify the task somehow.

Take preemptive breaks. If you know you typically drift after 20 minutes of sustained focus, take a 5-minute break at the 15-minute mark.

Match tasks to your current state. If you're in a drifty mood, choose tasks that require less sustained attention. Save the heavy focus work for when your brain is more cooperative.

Use the drift as information. If you consistently drift when working on certain projects, maybe those projects need to be broken down into smaller, more engaging pieces.

The goal isn't to eliminate drift completely—that's probably not possible for most ADHD brains. The goal is to catch it faster, understand what's causing it, and develop strategies to work with your brain's natural tendencies rather than against them.

Action Step

The drift isn't a failure of willpower—it's your brain's way of telling you it needs something different. Learning to notice and redirect drift with curiosity rather than criticism is a crucial ADHD skill.

For the next hour, set a gentle timer to go off every 10 minutes. When it chimes, simply notice: "Where is my attention right now?"

Don't try to change anything—just build your awareness of your own drift patterns. This awareness is the foundation for making conscious choices about where your attention goes.

Chapter 4: Catch and Interrupt the Focus Drift

The hardest part about losing focus isn't the losing part—it's the not noticing part.

I spent years drifting away from important tasks without realizing it was happening. I'd sit down to work on something meaningful, and three hours later I'd "wake up" having accomplished almost nothing, wondering where the time went and why I felt so frustrated.

There's a particular moment I remember with crystal clarity. I was working on an important article when I opened Twitter "just for a second" to check something work-related.

But instead of closing it, I found myself scrolling. Then I saw an interesting thread that led me to an article, which mentioned a book I wanted to remember, so I opened Amazon to bookmark it.

While there, I noticed they had a sale on notebooks, which reminded me that I needed to organize my current notebooks, so I got up to rearrange my bookshelf.

Twenty minutes later, I was standing in front of my bookshelf, holding a notebook from 2019, with absolutely no memory of how I'd gotten there or what I'd originally sat down to do.

That's when I realized I wasn't just dealing with occasional distraction. I was caught in a pattern of unconscious task-switching that was hijacking hours of my day without me even realizing it.

The breakthrough came when I understood two essential skills: **catching** the drift early and **interrupting** the loop before it takes over.

The Awareness Gap: Why We Don't Notice Drift

Here's what typically happens with ADHD brains: You start a task with good intentions and decent focus. Your attention begins to waver, but you don't notice this happening. You mentally or physically drift to something else.

Time passes—could be minutes or hours. Something jolts you back to awareness—a notification, a deadline, someone asking you a question. Finally, you realize you've been off-task and feel frustrated, guilty, or behind.

The gap between that initial waver and the eventual realization is where the magic happens. If you can learn to notice that moment when your focus starts to shift—before you're fully gone—you can choose what happens next instead of just letting it happen to you.

What Drift Actually Looks Like

Before you can catch drift, you need to recognize what it looks like in your own experience. Drift isn't always dramatic—often it's subtle, which is why it's so easy to miss.

Physical signs of drift:

- Your posture changes without you realizing it
- Your eyes lose focus or start scanning for something more interesting
- You start fidgeting or bouncing your leg
- Your breathing becomes shallow or irregular
- You reach for your phone without any conscious intention

Mental signs of drift:

- You realize you've been reading words without processing their meaning
- Your internal monologue goes quiet or becomes unfocused chatter

- You start thinking about things completely unrelated to your current task
- You can't remember what you just read or what you were about to do

Emotional signs of drift:

- You feel bored or restless, but can't quite put your finger on why
- There's a vague sense of dissatisfaction or resistance
- You feel drawn to "just check" something else—email, social media, the weather

Behavioral signs of drift:

- You reread the same paragraph multiple times without absorbing it
- You start doing task-adjacent activities— organizing your desk instead of writing
- You unconsciously open new browser tabs or apps
- You begin multitasking without deciding to

Understanding the Anatomy of a Loop

A loop isn't just one moment of distraction—it's a cascade of unconscious choices that build momentum over time. Here's how it typically unfolds:

You start with a clear intention, maybe even good focus. Then something pulls your attention away—a notification, a stray thought, a moment of boredom. Instead of catching this drift and redirecting, you follow the pull. That leads to another pull, then another, until you're six degrees of separation away from where you started, with no clear path back.

The cruel irony is that each individual switch feels justified in the moment. You're not deliberately sabotaging yourself. You're following a logical chain of associations that makes perfect sense to your ADHD brain: Check Twitter for work → see interesting thread → remember book → look up book → notice sale → think about organization → start organizing.

Each step feels productive, purposeful, even necessary. But the cumulative effect is that you've spent half an hour on everything except what you originally sat down to do.

Nasir's Drift Revelation

Nasir, a medical student with ADHD, kept falling behind in his coursework despite studying for what felt like hours each day.

"I'd sit down with my textbook at 7 PM, determined to learn the material," he shared in a forum post. "At midnight, I'd realize I'd only gotten through a few pages, but I couldn't explain where the time had gone."

Nasir started recording his study sessions with a simple time-lapse app on his phone. When he watched the footage, he was shocked. Every few minutes, his eyes would leave the page, he'd check his phone, or he'd stare into space. These micro-drifts were happening dozens of times per hour, but he had no awareness of them while they were occurring.

His breakthrough came when he began using what he called a "presence bell"—a simple app that chimed randomly every 5-10 minutes. When the bell sounded, he would ask himself: "Where is my attention right now?"

"At first, I was catching myself off-task about 80% of the time," he explained. "But just the act of noticing began to change things. After three weeks, I was staying on task more than half the time, and my comprehension improved dramatically."

What made this approach powerful wasn't that Nasir eliminated drift completely—that's probably impossible for an ADHD brain. It was that he reduced the duration of each drift by catching it earlier, before it could spiral into hours of lost time.

The Different Types of Loops

Not all loops look the same. Recognizing the different patterns can help you choose the right interruption strategy:

The Research Loop: You start looking up one simple fact and end up in a three-hour deep dive through Wikipedia, academic papers, and YouTube videos. Your brain loves learning, but it can't distinguish between relevant research and interesting tangents.

The Organization Loop: You sit down to work on a project but first decide to "quickly organize" your workspace, your files, your email, or your task list. Hours later, everything is beautifully organized, but your actual project is untouched.

The Social Loop: You check one message and end up scrolling through social media, reading articles people shared, watching videos, and engaging in discussions. Your brain craves social connection and interesting content, making it easy to get lost in these platforms.

The Perfectionist Loop: You start working on something, decide it's not quite right, and begin researching better methods, tools, or approaches. You spend more time optimizing your system than actually using it.

Building Your Drift Detection System

The good news is that you can train yourself to notice drift much earlier in the process. It's like developing a smoke detector for your attention—it alerts you to problems before they become fires.

I started with something simple: setting a gentle timer to go off every fifteen minutes. When it chimed, I would ask myself one question: "Where is my attention right now?" That's it. No judgment, no criticism, just data collection.

Your body often knows you're drifting before your mind does, so I also started doing quick physical check-ins:

- Am I still sitting the way I started?
- Is my breathing calm and regular?
- Are my hands and feet relaxed, or am I unconsciously tensing up?
- Is my gaze focused on what I'm supposed to be looking at?

Changes in your physical state often signal that your mental focus has shifted too. I learned that when my shoulders crept up toward my ears, it usually meant I was getting frustrated or overwhelmed.

When my breathing got shallow, it often meant I was anxious about the task I was working on. When I started slouching or leaning away from my work, it was usually a sign that my interest was waning.

The Moment of Power: Interrupting the Loop

Here's what I've learned about loops: the moment of maximum power isn't when you're deep in the loop—it's in the first few seconds after you've switched away from your original task.

There's a brief window, usually lasting just a few seconds, where your conscious mind can still override your brain's automatic pattern. It's like standing at the top of a hill with a snowball—once you let it roll, it's going to gain momentum and become much harder to stop.

The key is learning to recognize that moment and use it as an interruption point.

Indira's Wiki Wormhole

Indira, a UX designer with ADHD, described what she called her "wiki wormholes" with painful familiarity.

"I'd start researching a simple design question for a project, like 'best button placement for mobile screens,'" she explained. "Three hours later, I'd find myself reading about the history of cuneiform writing in ancient Mesopotamia, with 47 browser tabs open and my original question completely forgotten."

Her loops weren't random—they followed a predictable pattern of interesting connections. Button placement → eye-tracking studies → neuroscience of visual perception → evolution of human vision → ancient communication methods → cuneiform writing. Each step felt like legitimate research, but collectively, they took her far from her original goal.

The breakthrough came when Indira started using what she called a "research container." Before looking anything up, she would:

1. Write down her specific research question
2. Set a visual timer for 20 minutes

3. Open a fresh browser window with no other tabs
4. Start a voice recording on her phone saying "I'm researching button placement"

The timer provided an external interrupt to the loop, but it was the voice recording that proved most powerful. "Hearing my own voice stating my original intention created this moment of 'oh right, that's what I was doing,'" Indira explained. "It broke the trance of the loop."

Using this simple container strategy, Indira was able to reduce her research loops from hours to minutes. She still occasionally went down interesting rabbit holes, but now it was a conscious choice rather than an unconscious drift.

The Loop Interrupt Toolkit

After years of experimentation, I've developed a simple but effective toolkit for breaking loops before they take over my day:

The Five-Second Pause: When you notice you're about to switch tasks, count slowly to five before making the switch. This creates just enough space for your conscious mind to engage. Often, you'll realize the switch isn't actually necessary.

The Intention Check: Before switching, ask yourself: "What was I originally trying to accomplish?" This reconnects you with your initial purpose and helps you evaluate whether the switch serves that purpose or derails it.

The Write-It-Down Method: When your brain wants to switch to handle something else, write down the thing you want to do instead of doing it immediately. This satisfies your brain's need to capture the thought while allowing you to stay with your current task.

The Physical Reset: Stand up, take three deep breaths, and move your body for thirty seconds. This interrupts the neural pattern of the loop and gives you a fresh start point.

The Gentle Redirect: When you catch yourself drifting, don't panic or launch into self-criticism. Instead, practice this four-step process:

1. **Acknowledge:** "Oh, I notice my attention has wandered."
2. **Get curious:** "What was I thinking about? What was my brain seeking?"
3. **Choose consciously:** "What do I want to focus on now?"

4.   **Re-engage:** Either return to your chosen task or consciously choose a different one.

My Current Drift-Interrupt System

After years of refinement, my system for catching and interrupting drift has become second nature. I start each work session by clearly stating—out loud—what I plan to focus on and for how long. This creates what psychologists call an "implementation intention," which makes it easier to notice when I've deviated from my chosen path.

I keep a small smooth stone on my desk as a physical anchor. When I feel my attention starting to waver, I touch the stone. The tactile sensation helps bring me back to the present moment and reminds me to check in with my focus.

I set gentle timers, but I've learned to adjust the intervals based on the type of work I'm doing and my current mental state. For challenging creative work, I might set it for twenty minutes. For routine tasks, maybe thirty. On days when I'm feeling particularly scattered, I might use ten-minute intervals.

When I notice myself about to follow a distraction loop, I use the five-second pause and ask: "What was I originally trying to accomplish?" This simple question reconnects me with my initial purpose and often prevents unnecessary task-switching.

At the end of each workday, I spend a few minutes reflecting on when I felt most focused and when I drifted most. This isn't for self-judgment—it's for pattern recognition. Over time, these reflections have helped me understand my own rhythms and plan better for future days.

When Loops Serve a Purpose

Here's something counterintuitive: sometimes loops are actually serving an important function, and trying to force yourself out of them creates more problems than it solves.

Sometimes a research loop happens because you genuinely need more information before you can proceed effectively. Sometimes an organization loop emerges because your workspace or systems really are too chaotic to support focused work. Sometimes a social loop occurs because you're feeling isolated and need human connection.

The key is learning to distinguish between loops that serve a purpose and loops that are just your brain seeking stimulation or avoiding difficult work.

I've developed what I call the "Loop Audit" question: "Is this loop moving me toward my larger goal, or is it moving me away from it?"

If I'm researching background information that will genuinely help me write better, that might be a productive loop. If I'm reorganizing my digital files to avoid starting a challenging project, that's probably an avoidance loop.

Action Step

Drift isn't a failure of willpower—it's your brain's way of telling you it needs something different.

Build your awareness by setting a gentle timer to go off every 15 minutes. When it chimes, simply notice: "Where is my attention right now?" Then apply the five-second pause before switching tasks.

This simple practice starts building your drift detection system while giving you the momentary space to choose your response rather than automatically following distractions.

SECTION 2:
Core Reset Techniques

Chapter 5: Anchor to One Thing—The Power of Micro-Actions

There's a moment that happens when you've successfully interrupted a loop or caught yourself drifting. You're standing at a crossroads, fully aware that your attention has wandered, ready to make a conscious choice about what to do next.

And then... nothing.

You stare at your to-do list, or your computer screen, or the project you were supposed to be working on, and suddenly everything feels equally urgent, equally overwhelming, or equally meaningless. Your brain, which just moments ago was happily bouncing between seventeen different tasks, now can't seem to land on any single thing.

This is what I call "the restart paralysis"—that moment when you know you need to refocus, but you can't figure out where to begin. It's like your brain's GPS has recalculated your route but can't decide which direction to point you.

For years, this moment defeated me. I'd successfully catch myself in a drift or break out of a loop, feel proud of my awareness, and then... stand there, paralyzed by choice, until I eventually drifted away again.

The solution, I discovered, wasn't to make a perfect choice or to tackle the most important thing. It was to make the smallest possible choice and build momentum from there.

The Overwhelm of Re-Entry

When you're trying to refocus after a period of drift or distraction, your ADHD brain faces a perfect storm of challenges.

First, there's decision fatigue. You've just spent mental energy noticing your drift and interrupting your loop. Now you're asking your already-tired executive function to make another decision about what to focus on next.

Second, there's the magnitude problem. When you look at your original task after being away from it, it often feels bigger and more overwhelming than when you started. Your brain has forgotten the momentum you had built, and the work ahead looks like an insurmountable mountain.

Third, there's what I call "choice paralysis." When you're not actively engaged in something, every option looks equally valid or equally unappealing.

Should you return to your original task? Handle something urgent that just came up? Take a break? Switch to something easier? Your brain can't decide, so it doesn't decide.

The result is that you end up standing in mental quicksand, aware that you should be doing something but unable to choose what, until eventually your brain gives up and wanders off again.

My Breakthrough with Micro-Actions

The discovery that changed my entire approach to refocusing came during a particularly frustrating writing session.

I was working on a chapter that felt impossibly complex. Every time I tried to restart after a distraction, I'd look at the document and feel overwhelmed by how much I still needed to write, how many ideas I needed to organize, how many decisions I needed to make about structure and flow.

Finally, in a moment of desperation, I decided to set the bar ridiculously low. Instead of trying to write the entire section, or even a good paragraph, I committed to writing just one sentence. Not a perfect sentence. Not a sentence that would stay in the final draft. Just any sentence that moved me one tiny step forward.

"The human brain is weird," I typed.

It wasn't elegant. It wasn't profound. But it was something. And somehow, having that one sentence on the page made writing the next sentence feel possible. Then the next. Within twenty minutes, I had written three paragraphs and was back in a flow state.

That's when I understood the power of what I now call "micro-actions"—tasks so small that your brain can't find a reason to resist them.

What Makes a Good Micro-Action

An effective micro-action has several key characteristics that make it perfect for ADHD brains trying to refocus:

It's ridiculously small. We're talking 30 seconds to 2 minutes maximum. The goal is to choose something so small that even your most resistance-prone brain can't object to it.

It's concrete and specific. "Work on the presentation" is not a micro-action. "Open the presentation document and read the first slide" is a micro-action. Vague tasks create decision fatigue; specific tasks create momentum.

It requires minimal decision-making. Good micro-actions are so clear that you don't have to think about how to do them. They're pure execution, not planning or strategizing.

It connects to your larger goal. This isn't busywork or procrastination disguised as productivity. It's the smallest possible step toward what you actually want to accomplish.

It feels achievable in your current state. If you're mentally foggy, don't choose a micro-action that requires sharp thinking. If you're restless, don't choose something that requires sitting still. Match the action to your current capacity.

Sanjay's Sentence Strategy

I read about Sanjay, a novelist with ADHD, who struggled with the daunting task of writing a full-length book. He would sit down with ambitions of writing for hours, only to find himself paralyzed by the magnitude of what he was attempting.

"I'd stare at the blank page thinking about the 80,000 words I needed to write, and my brain would just shut down," he explained in an interview. "It was like trying to climb a mountain by looking at the summit the entire time."

Sanjay's breakthrough came when he developed what he called his "Just One Sentence" strategy. Instead of trying to write for a certain amount of time or produce a specific word count, he committed to writing exactly one sentence each time he sat down.

"The sentence could be terrible. It could be something I'd definitely delete later. It just had to be one sentence about my story," he shared.

The strategy worked for two reasons. First, it was so absurdly small that his brain couldn't find a reason to resist it. Second, once he wrote that first sentence, he almost always felt like writing a second one, and then a third.

"Some days I'd write just the one sentence and walk away. But most days, that tiny action would break the paralysis, and I'd end up writing for an hour or more," Sanjay explained.

Using this micro-action approach, he completed his novel in fourteen months—while holding down a full-time job and raising two young children. The key wasn't superhuman focus or rigid discipline; it was recognizing that the smallest possible step was often the most powerful one.

The Micro-Action Menu

Over the years, I've developed a menu of go-to micro-actions for different types of work. When I'm struggling to refocus, I don't have to invent a new approach—I just choose from my existing menu based on what type of work I'm doing and what my brain feels capable of in the moment.

For writing projects:

- Read the last paragraph I wrote

- Write one terrible sentence

- Add one bullet point to my outline

For administrative tasks:

- Open the relevant document

- Read one email

- Write down the first step of the process

For creative projects:

- Look at the last thing I created

- Sketch one rough idea

- Gather one piece of reference material

For learning or research:

- Read one paragraph

- Watch two minutes of a video

- Write down one question I want to answer

The key is having these options ready ahead of time, so when you're in that overwhelmed restart moment, you don't have to invent a new approach. You just choose the smallest thing from your menu and do it.

Why Micro-Actions Work for ADHD Brains

There's solid neuroscience behind why micro-actions are so effective for people with ADHD.

They bypass the executive function bottleneck. When a task feels big or complex, your prefrontal cortex—already struggling with ADHD-related challenges—has to work overtime to plan, organize, and initiate. Micro-actions are so simple they can often run on autopilot.

They provide immediate dopamine. Completing something, even something tiny, gives your brain a small hit of satisfaction and accomplishment. This reward reinforces the focusing behavior and makes the next small step feel more appealing.

They create what psychologists call "behavioral momentum." An object in motion stays in motion. Once you've taken one small action, taking the next small action feels easier than stopping.

They reduce the emotional weight of the task. Big projects can trigger anxiety, perfectionism, or overwhelm. Small actions feel emotionally neutral, which lets you engage with the work without fighting your emotional resistance.

They build evidence of your capability. Every micro-action you complete is proof that you can follow through, even when things feel difficult. This builds self-trust and reduces the anxiety that often accompanies task initiation.

My Personal Micro-Action Ritual

When I catch myself drifting or successfully break out of a loop, I've developed a simple ritual that almost always gets me re-engaged with meaningful work.

First, I pause and take one conscious breath. This creates a moment of space between the drift and the re-engagement.

Then I ask myself: "What's the smallest thing I could do right now that would move me toward what I care about?" Not the most important thing, not the most urgent thing—the smallest thing that connects to something meaningful.

Finally, I commit to doing just that one thing, with permission to stop after I complete it. Usually, I don't want to stop. But giving myself permission to stop removes the psychological pressure that often creates resistance.

This entire process takes about thirty seconds, but it's become my most reliable tool for getting back on track when my focus has wandered.

When Micro-Actions Feel Too Small

Sometimes people worry that micro-actions are just a way of avoiding real work or making ourselves feel productive without actually accomplishing anything significant.

I understand this concern, but in my experience, it's based on a misunderstanding of how momentum works for ADHD brains.

For neurotypical brains, it might make sense to push through resistance and tackle big chunks of work through discipline and willpower. But ADHD brains often work better with an approach that feels more like gentle persistence than forceful effort.

I've written entire books using micro-actions. Not every writing session was a micro-action, but on the days when my brain felt scattered or resistant, choosing to write just one sentence or edit just one paragraph kept me connected to the project and often led to much more substantial work.

The goal of a micro-action isn't to complete your entire project in tiny increments. It's to maintain connection and momentum so that when your brain is ready for deeper focus, you don't have to overcome the inertia of having been away from the work.

> **Action Step:** When you're struggling to refocus, the answer isn't to tackle the biggest or most important task. It's to choose the smallest action that connects to what you care about and build momentum from there.
>
> Think of one project or task you've been avoiding or struggling to restart.
>
> Write down three micro-actions—each taking less than two minutes—that would move you one tiny step forward. Then do the smallest one right now.

Chapter 6: Reset Your Space—Make Your Environment Work for You

I used to think my workspace chaos was just a quirky personality trait.

My desk was an archaeological dig of half-finished projects, old coffee cups, random notebooks, charging cables, and those mysterious piles of papers that I was definitely going to organize "someday."

I had seventeen browser tabs open at any given moment, my desktop was covered with files I'd saved "temporarily," and my phone sat right next to my keyboard, buzzing with notifications throughout the day.

I told myself this was creative messiness. That I worked better in organized chaos. That I knew where everything was, even if it looked disorganized to other people.

But here's what I didn't realize: every single item in my visual field was making a tiny claim on my attention. Every notification was interrupting my thought process. Every cluttered surface was subtly increasing my stress levels and making it harder for my ADHD brain to settle into focused work.

The breakthrough came during a particularly frustrating week when I couldn't seem to focus on anything for more than ten minutes.

In desperation, I cleared everything off my desk except my laptop, a notebook, and a pen. I closed all but one browser tab. I put my phone in another room.

The difference was immediate and dramatic. My brain felt calmer. My thoughts felt clearer. I could actually think without part of my attention being pulled toward all the visual noise around me.

That's when I understood something crucial: **for ADHD brains, environment isn't just background—it's foreground.** Every element in your workspace is either supporting your focus or stealing it.

Why Environment Hits ADHD Brains Harder

ADHD brains process sensory information differently than neurotypical brains. We have what researchers call "sensory gating" difficulties—we struggle to filter out irrelevant stimuli and focus on what's important. This means that background noise, visual clutter, movement, and other environmental factors that neurotypical people can easily ignore continue to demand our attention.

Think of it this way: if a neurotypical brain is like having selective hearing that can tune out conversations in a crowded restaurant, an ADHD brain is like having supersonic hearing that picks up every conversation, every dish clinking, every footstep, every air conditioning hum. All of that information is competing for the same limited attention resources you need for your actual work.

This isn't just about being "easily distracted." It's about cognitive load. Every piece of visual clutter, every notification, every unfinished task visible in your peripheral vision is using up mental energy that could be directed toward your primary focus.

The Day I Realized My Desk Was Sabotaging Me

The moment everything clicked for me happened during a writing session that should have been straightforward. I was working on an article with a clear outline and plenty of material. But I kept getting stuck, losing my train of thought, and feeling frustrated.

After an hour of struggling, I noticed something: every few minutes, my eyes would unconsciously scan the objects on my desk. The stack of bills I needed to pay. The book I'd been meaning to read. The broken headphones I'd been meaning to fix. The coffee mug from three days ago that I'd been meaning to wash.

Each glance was tiny—maybe half a second—but each one created a micro-interruption in my thinking. My brain would see the bills and momentarily worry about finances. It would see the book and wonder if I should be reading instead of writing. It would see the broken headphones and add "fix headphones" to the mental to-do list running in the background.

None of these thoughts were conscious or deliberate, but they were happening dozens of times throughout my work session, fragmenting my attention and making sustained focus nearly impossible.

I spent the next twenty minutes clearing my desk completely. Not organizing it—clearing it. Everything went into a box that I moved to another room. When I returned to writing, the difference was remarkable. My thoughts felt more linear. My attention felt more stable. I wrote more in the next hour than I had in the previous three.

The Hidden Attention Thieves

Once I started paying attention to how my environment affected my focus, I began noticing attention thieves everywhere:

Visual noise that I'd learned to ignore but that was still processing in my peripheral vision. Every poster on the wall, every decorative object, every stack of papers was subtly competing for my attention. My brain was constantly making micro-decisions about whether each item was important or could be ignored.

Digital chaos was even worse. Those seventeen browser tabs weren't just taking up screen space—they were taking up mental space. Each tab represented an unfinished thought, an incomplete task, a potential distraction.

Part of my brain was always tracking them, wondering if one of them might be more important or interesting than what I was currently working on.

Notifications were the worst attention thieves of all. Even when I told myself I could ignore them, the mere knowledge that my phone might buzz at any moment kept part of my attention in a state of anticipation. I wasn't fully present with my work because part of me was always listening for the next ping.

Ambient noise that I thought I'd tuned out was actually creating constant low-level stress. Conversations in the next room, traffic outside, the hum of appliances—all of it was being processed by my brain and requiring energy to filter out.

Even **organizational systems** that were supposed to help me focus were sometimes working against me. Complex filing systems, elaborate color-coding schemes, and productivity apps with too many features all required mental energy to navigate and maintain.

Ximena's Environmental Transformation

I read about Ximena, a graphic designer with ADHD, who struggled with consistent productivity despite having a beautiful home office with all the latest ergonomic furniture and technology.

"I'd spent thousands on the perfect desk, chair, and monitor setup," she explained in an online forum. "But I was still having days where I couldn't focus for more than ten minutes at a time."

When Ximena started tracking her productivity patterns, she noticed something surprising: she often did her best work at the local library or in simple coffee shops with minimal decor.

This realization led her to completely rethink her workspace. She removed all decorative objects from her desk and walls. She replaced her multi-monitor setup with a single screen. She created what she called a "focus wall"—the wall her desk faced was completely blank except for a simple clock.

"The difference was immediate and dramatic," she shared. "Without all the visual stimulation competing for my attention, my brain could finally settle into deep focus."

Ximena's story illustrates an important principle for ADHD brains: sometimes less stimulation creates more mental space for the work that matters.

Creating Your Focus Sanctuary

The solution isn't to work in a completely sterile environment—that can be understimulating for ADHD brains. It's about being intentional with every element in your workspace so that everything either supports your focus or gets removed.

I started with what I call the "single-task surface" principle. My desk now has only what I need for my current task, nothing more. If I'm writing, it's laptop, notebook, pen, and water. If I'm doing administrative work, it's laptop and the specific documents I'm working with. Everything else lives somewhere else.

This felt extreme at first. I worried I'd forget about important things if they weren't visible. But I discovered that having fewer things visible actually made the important things more prominent, not less.

When there are only three items on your desk, you notice each one. When there are twenty-three items, your brain starts to treat them all as background noise.

I applied the same principle to my digital environment. One browser tab per task. One document open at a time. Phone in a different room during focused work sessions. Email closed unless I'm specifically handling email.

For background sound, I experimented until I found what worked for my brain. Complete silence was sometimes too understimulating. Music with lyrics was too distracting. But instrumental music, nature sounds, or white noise at a low volume helped mask environmental distractions without creating new ones.

The 5-Minute Environment Reset

I developed a simple ritual that I use before any focused work session. I call it the 5-minute environment reset, and it's become one of my most valuable productivity tools.

First, I clear my visual field. Everything that's not directly related to my current task gets moved out of sight. This isn't about permanent organization—it's about temporary focus. The bills can go back on my desk after I finish writing. But while I'm writing, they live in a drawer.

Next, I set up my digital environment for single-tasking. One browser window, one tab, one document. Everything else gets closed or minimized. I turn off all notifications except true emergencies.

Then I optimize for my current needs. If I need to think deeply, I might put on noise-canceling headphones with brown noise. If I need to brainstorm, I might open the window for fresh air and natural light. If I need to power through administrative tasks, I might put on energizing music.

I create physical boundaries for the work session. This might mean closing the door, putting up a "do not disturb" sign, or simply turning my chair so I'm facing away from high-traffic areas.

Finally, I set an intention for the space. I take one conscious breath in my reset environment and remind myself what I'm here to accomplish.

This entire process takes less than five minutes, but it consistently doubles or triples my focus and productivity for the session that follows.

When Less Becomes More

One of the most surprising discoveries in my environment experiments was how much creative energy I was using to navigate clutter and complexity. When I simplified my workspace, I didn't just reduce distractions—I freed up mental energy for actual creative thinking.

I noticed this most dramatically when I started using what I call "project boxes." Instead of keeping all my current projects visible on my desk, I put each project's materials in a separate box. When I wanted to work on something, I'd clear my desk completely and take out just that one box.

Initially, this felt like it would slow me down. Wouldn't it be more efficient to have everything accessible at once? But I discovered the opposite was true. Having fewer choices paradoxically made me more decisive. Having less visual information allowed me to process relevant information more quickly and clearly.

The same principle applied to my digital tools. I went from using seventeen different productivity apps to using three simple ones well. Instead of having hundreds of files on my desktop, I created a simple folder structure and disciplined myself to put things where they belonged immediately.

This wasn't about becoming a minimalist for minimalism's sake. It was about recognizing that my ADHD brain works better with less information to process at any given moment.

Action Step: Your environment is either supporting your focus or stealing it—there's no neutral.

ADHD brains are especially sensitive to environmental factors, making it crucial to be intentional about your workspace.

Look around your current workspace and identify three things that aren't directly related to what you're trying to accomplish right now.

Move them out of your visual field, even if just temporarily. Notice how this affects your ability to think and focus.

Chapter 7: Close the Loop— Finish Strong, Start Fresh

There's a special kind of exhaustion that comes from working hard all day but having nothing concrete to show for it.

You know the feeling. You've been busy for eight hours straight. You've answered emails, attended meetings, started projects, made progress on various tasks. But when someone asks "What did you accomplish today?" you struggle to give a clear answer.

This is what happens when you never close loops.

> *"The human brain is not designed to remember incomplete tasks—it's designed to worry about them." — David Allen*

For ADHD brains, this problem is amplified tenfold. We're natural starters but reluctant finishers. We love the excitement of beginning something new but often struggle with the less glamorous work of completion.

As a result, we accumulate dozens of half-finished projects that take up mental space and emotional energy long after we've moved on to something else.

Learning to close loops—to create clear endings and beginnings—might be the single most important skill for maintaining both productivity and peace of mind with an ADHD brain.

The Mental Load of Open Loops

An open loop is anything you've started but haven't finished or properly put aside. It's the email you read but didn't respond to. The book you're halfway through but haven't touched in weeks. The project you got excited about but abandoned when something more interesting came along. The conversation you meant to follow up on but forgot about.

Each open loop creates what psychologists call a "Zeigarnik effect"—your brain continues to allocate mental resources to incomplete tasks, even when you're not consciously thinking about them. It's like having dozens of browser tabs open in the background of your mind, each one using up a little bit of your mental processing power.

I discovered just how much mental load I was carrying when I did what I call an "open loop audit." I spent an hour listing everything I had started but not finished or properly concluded. The list was staggering.

There were seventeen books I was "currently reading." Five online courses I had started but never completed. Twelve personal projects in various stages of incompletion. Twenty-three emails I had read but not responded to. Three subscriptions to magazines I never read but felt guilty about canceling. Two half-written blog posts. One bathroom renovation that had been "almost done" for six months.

Just writing the list was exhausting. But it also explained why I often felt mentally cluttered and unable to focus, even when my schedule wasn't particularly busy.

My Loop-Closing Awakening

The moment I realized how much open loops were affecting my mental clarity came during a particularly scattered week when I couldn't seem to finish anything I started.

I would sit down to work on Project A, remember something I needed to do for Project B, start working on that, get interrupted by an email about Project C, begin responding to that, remember I hadn't finished reading an article related to Project D, open that up, and so on.

By Thursday of that week, I felt like my brain was a pinball machine with seventeen balls bouncing around simultaneously. I couldn't think clearly about any single thing because part of my attention was always being pulled toward all the other unfinished things.

That evening, I decided to try something radical: I was going to close as many loops as possible before starting anything new.

I spent two hours going through my open loops systematically:

Quick completions: I finished and sent the three emails that only needed brief responses. I returned the library book I'd been carrying around for weeks. I ordered the replacement part for the broken appliance instead of continuing to work around it.

Clear decisions: I officially abandoned two projects that I'd been halfheartedly working on but wasn't actually excited about. I unsubscribed from newsletters I never read. I deleted the half-written blog posts that no longer felt relevant.

Proper parking: For projects I wanted to continue but couldn't finish immediately, I created clear "parking spaces"—specific notes about where I left off and what the next step would be when I returned.

The mental relief was immediate and profound. It felt like someone had defragmented my brain's hard drive. Suddenly I could think clearly about individual tasks without feeling the constant background pressure of everything else I wasn't doing.

The Anatomy of a Proper Loop Closure

Closing a loop isn't just about finishing something—it's about creating a clear endpoint that allows your brain to let go and move on. Different types of loops require different types of closure.

Completion closure is the gold standard—you actually finish the task or project. You send the email, complete the assignment, publish the article, have the difficult conversation. Your brain gets the satisfaction of genuine accomplishment and can fully disengage from the task.

Decision closure happens when you consciously choose not to continue with something. Maybe you realize a project isn't worth pursuing, or a book isn't worth finishing, or a commitment doesn't align with your current priorities. The key is making the decision explicitly rather than just letting things fade away through neglect.

Parking closure is for tasks you want to continue but can't finish right now. You create a clear record of where you left off, what you've accomplished so far, and what the next steps would be. This allows your brain to let go of the task without losing the work you've already invested.

Handoff closure occurs when you transfer responsibility for something to someone else. You delegate a task, refer someone to a different resource, or acknowledge that something is outside your area of responsibility. The loop closes for you even though it continues for someone else.

Reza's Closure Ritual

I read about Reza, a product manager with ADHD, who described himself as "the king of almost-done." He would get projects to about

90% completion and then struggle to finish the final details.

"I had a graveyard of nearly-finished projects, both at work and in my personal life," he explained in an article. "The last 10% felt boring and tedious compared to the excitement of starting something new."

The mental weight of all these open loops was creating constant background stress. Reza could never fully enjoy his free time because part of his brain was always thinking about all the things he hadn't quite finished.

His breakthrough came when he developed what he called his "Friday Closure Ritual." Every Friday afternoon, he would dedicate the last hour of his workday to closing loops. He had three categories:

Micro-completions: Small tasks he could finish in 10 minutes or less. He would batch these together and power through as many as possible.

Decision points: Projects that had been lingering for too long. For each one, he would decide: complete it today, schedule a specific time to finish it next week, or officially abandon it.

Transition notes: For ongoing projects, he would write a clear summary of the current status and specific next steps, so he could pick up exactly where he left off.

"This ritual changed everything for me," Reza shared. "I stopped carrying the mental weight of dozens of unfinished tasks into my weekend. I started each Monday with clarity instead of dread."

Within a few months of implementing this practice, Reza's reputation at work transformed from someone who generated great ideas but couldn't follow through to someone known for reliable execution. But the biggest benefit was personal—the constant mental noise of open loops had diminished, allowing him to be more present both at work and at home.

The Evening Loop Review

One of the most transformative habits I've developed is what I call the "evening loop review." Every day before I stop working, I spend five minutes identifying any loops I've opened during the day and deciding how to handle them.

This isn't about forcing myself to finish everything—that would be impossible and counterproductive. It's about making conscious choices about what stays open and what gets closed.

Today's completions: What did I actually finish? I celebrate these, even if they seem small. Acknowledging completions reinforces the satisfaction of closure and motivates future finishing behavior.

Tomorrow's priorities: What open loops are most important to continue tomorrow? I choose no more than three and write down the specific next action for each one.

Conscious parkings: What projects am I putting aside temporarily? I make a brief note about the current status and file it where I can find it later.

Deliberate closures: What am I choosing not to continue? I make this decision explicit rather than letting things die by neglect.

This five-minute practice has dramatically reduced my mental clutter and increased my sense of control over my work and commitments.

When Starting Feels Better Than Finishing

One of the biggest challenges for ADHD brains is that starting almost always feels better than finishing. Beginning something new provides novelty, possibility, and excitement. Finishing something often involves tedious details, quality control, and the recognition that the result isn't as perfect as you imagined it could be.

I used to think this meant I was just lazy or lacked follow-through. But I've come to understand it as a neurological reality that requires conscious strategies to manage.

The key insight was recognizing that my brain needed the reward of completion to stay motivated for finishing tasks. I started building artificial completion rewards into my projects by breaking them into smaller segments that each had their own sense of closure.

Instead of "write the article," I would have subtasks like "complete the outline," "write the introduction," "finish the first section," and so on. Each completion gave me a small hit of satisfaction and momentum for the next piece.

I also learned to make the act of finishing more rewarding by creating simple ceremonies around completion. When I finish a project, I do something to mark the moment—update my project list, send myself a congratulatory email, or even just say "Done!" out loud. These small rituals help my brain register the completion and get the neurochemical reward that reinforces finishing behavior.

The Art of Strategic Abandonment

Not everything deserves to be finished. Learning to abandon projects strategically—rather than just letting them fade away through neglect—is a crucial skill for managing mental bandwidth.

I've developed what I call the "completion criteria" for evaluating whether something is worth finishing:

Does it still align with my current goals and priorities? Projects that made sense six months ago might not make sense today, and that's okay.

Am I still genuinely interested in it, or am I just continuing out of obligation? Forcing yourself to finish something you've lost interest in is often less productive than consciously choosing to stop and redirect that energy elsewhere.

What would finishing it require, and is that a good use of my current resources? Sometimes the cost of completion—in time, energy, or opportunity cost—outweighs the benefits.

What would happen if I didn't finish it? Often, the consequences of not finishing something are much smaller than we imagine.

When I decide to abandon a project, I make it official. I write a brief note about why I'm stopping, what I learned from the experience, and whether there are any elements worth salvaging for future projects. This transforms abandonment from a failure into a conscious choice and valuable learning experience.

Creating Finishing Momentum

The more you practice closing loops, the easier it becomes. Completion creates momentum for more completion, just as starting creates momentum for more starting.

I noticed this most clearly when I started doing what I call "completion sprints"—dedicated time blocks where I focus solely on finishing small, lingering tasks. During these sprints, I'm not allowed to start anything new, only complete things that are already in progress.

These sessions are incredibly satisfying because they create multiple completion experiences in a short time. Each finished task makes the next one feel more achievable. By the end of a completion sprint, I feel energized and capable rather than scattered and overwhelmed.

Some of my favorite loop-closing practices include:

Monday morning loop cleanup: I spend the first 30 minutes of each week closing any loops that accumulated over the weekend and creating clear starting points for the week ahead.

Friday afternoon completions: I use the last hour of each work week to finish small lingering tasks and create clear endpoints for projects that will continue next week.

Monthly project audit: Once a month, I review all my ongoing projects and make conscious decisions about what to continue, what to park, and what to abandon.

> **Action Step:** Open loops consume mental energy even when you're not actively thinking about them. Learning to close loops consciously—through completion, decision, or proper parking—frees up cognitive

resources for focused work. Make a list of three tasks you started but haven't finished.

Choose one to complete today, one to officially abandon, and one to "park" with a clear note about where you left off.

Notice how it feels to make these conscious decisions rather than letting things remain in limbo.

Chapter 8: Morning Reset—Start Without the Avalanche

The first twenty minutes of my day used to feel like being buried alive.

Before I was even fully awake, my brain would start downloading the day's anxieties: the project deadline looming, the email I forgot to send yesterday, the meeting I wasn't prepared for, the seventeen different directions I could take my work, and the crushing awareness that I had approximately forty-seven important things to do and no clear sense of which one to tackle first.

By the time I sat down with my coffee, I was already mentally exhausted from trying to hold all these competing priorities in my head simultaneously. I'd open my laptop feeling overwhelmed before I'd even started working.

I called this the "morning avalanche"—that overwhelming rush of tasks, worries, and possibilities that would crash down on me the moment I became conscious. For years, I thought this was just how mornings worked when you had a lot of responsibilities.

"How you start your morning shapes your entire day. For ADHD brains, this is especially true—we set the tone for our attention and energy in those first few minutes."

Then I discovered something that changed everything: I could interrupt the avalanche before it gained momentum.

The ADHD Morning Brain

ADHD brains are particularly vulnerable in the morning because we're trying to come online while simultaneously processing all the information we've been accumulating since we last worked. It's like trying to boot up an old computer that has seventeen programs trying to launch at startup.

Your working memory, already limited by ADHD, gets flooded with everything that feels urgent or important. Your executive function, which hasn't fully activated yet, struggles to prioritize and organize all this information. Your emotional regulation system, still warming up, can get overwhelmed by the sheer volume of things that need attention.

The result is that you feel behind before you've even started. You feel scattered before you've attempted to focus. You feel overwhelmed before you've tackled a single task.

I used to think the solution was to push through this feeling, to power up faster and get moving more quickly. But I learned that the opposite approach—slowing down the startup process—was far more effective.

My Morning Avalanche Breaking Point

The morning that changed everything was a Tuesday in March when I had a particularly important client presentation to prepare. I'd been putting it off for days, and now I had exactly three hours to pull together something that should have taken me a week to create properly.

I woke up with my heart already racing. Before I'd even gotten out of bed, my brain was spiraling through everything I needed to do: research the client's industry, update my existing presentation template, practice my delivery, prepare for potential questions, check my calendar for conflicts, respond to urgent emails, and somehow also handle all the regular Tuesday tasks that couldn't be ignored.

By the time I sat down at my computer, I was in full panic mode. I opened seven different documents simultaneously, started three different research processes, and began responding to emails while also trying to outline my presentation. Within twenty minutes, I had made progress on nothing and felt completely paralyzed.

That's when I realized I was sabotaging myself before I'd even started. The avalanche wasn't helping me prepare—it was burying me under anxiety and scattered attention.

I closed everything, took five deep breaths, and asked myself one simple question: "What's the single most important thing I need to accomplish in the next hour?"

The answer was obvious: create a rough outline for the presentation. Not perfect slides, not comprehensive research, not a flawless delivery—just a basic structure that would give me something to build on.

I spent the next hour working on nothing but that outline. When it was done, I had a clear foundation and a much calmer nervous system. The rest of the preparation flowed naturally from there.

The Power of the Single Starting Point

The key insight from that morning was that ADHD brains need a single, clear starting point rather than multiple competing priorities. When you try to hold seventeen important things in your mind simultaneously, your brain can't choose any of them effectively.

But when you identify one clear starting point— not necessarily the most important thing, but the most logical first step—your brain can engage its focus and build momentum from there.

This doesn't mean ignoring everything else. It means acknowledging everything else while choosing one thing to begin with. The other tasks don't disappear; they just stop competing for your immediate attention.

I started experimenting with what I call the "single point start." Every morning, before I looked at my email, my calendar, or my task list,

I would choose one specific thing to work on first. Not the most urgent thing, not the most important thing, but the thing that felt most manageable and momentum-building.

Sometimes it was a creative task that required fresh mental energy. Sometimes it was a simple administrative task that would give me a quick win. Sometimes it was just reading and responding to one specific email that I'd been avoiding.

The key was that I chose consciously rather than reactively. Instead of letting the avalanche choose my starting point, I took control of my own beginning.

Olivia's Morning Tile System

I read about Olivia, a teacher with ADHD, who described her mornings as "waking up already behind." With a classroom full of children waiting for her, she couldn't afford the scattered starts that had become her pattern.

"I'd arrive at school with my brain in seventeen different places," she explained in an educational forum. "I'd forget materials I needed, start activities without clear directions, and spend the first hour playing catch-up with myself."

Olivia's breakthrough came when she developed what she called her "One Tile" system. Each evening before leaving school, she would create a single index card with exactly one morning task written on it—the first thing she needed to do when she arrived the next day. She would place this card in the center of her desk where she couldn't miss it.

"The tile had to be something small and specific," she shared. "Not 'prepare for math lesson' but 'set out the fraction manipulatives and make copies of worksheet A.'"

When she arrived each morning, the single tile was waiting. She wasn't allowed to check email, talk to colleagues, or start any other task until she had completed just that one specific action.

"It sounds so simple, but it completely transformed my mornings," Olivia explained. "That one completed task created a sense of calm and accomplishment that set the tone for the entire day."

Over time, Olivia expanded her system to include a second tile that she could turn to after completing the first. But she was careful to never have more than two tiles visible at once. This strict limitation forced her to prioritize effectively and prevented the overwhelming avalanche of options that had previously derailed her mornings.

My Current Morning Reset Ritual

After years of refining this approach, my morning reset has become a simple but powerful ritual that consistently sets me up for focused, productive days.

The First Five Minutes: Before I check any external inputs—email, messages, news, social media—I spend five minutes reconnecting with my own intentions. I ask myself three questions:

- What do I want to accomplish today that would make me feel good about how I spent my time?

- What's my energy level right now, and what type of work does that suggest?

- What's one specific task I could start with that would build momentum for the rest of the day?

I write down brief answers to these questions, not because I need a permanent record, but because the act of writing helps my brain organize and prioritize.

The Single Task Choice: Based on my answers, I choose one specific task to begin with. I write it down in large letters on a sticky note and put it where I can see it. This becomes my anchor point—if I get distracted or overwhelmed, I can return to this single, clear intention.

The Environment Setup: I prepare my workspace for focused work on that one task. This means closing unnecessary browser tabs, clearing my desk of unrelated items, and removing or silencing potential distractions.

The 25-Minute Sprint: I set a timer for 25 minutes and work on nothing but my chosen task. If other things come to mind, I jot them down on a separate piece of paper but don't act on them until the timer goes off.

The Momentum Decision: When the timer rings, I have a choice. I can continue with the same task if I'm in a flow state, or I can consciously choose what to do next based on what I've accomplished and how I'm feeling.

This entire ritual takes about 30 minutes, but it consistently prevents the morning avalanche and sets me up for a day of intentional rather than reactive work.

When the Avalanche Hits Anyway

Some mornings, despite your best intentions, the avalanche still happens. You wake up anxious, or you get hit with an urgent crisis, or you simply can't shake the feeling that everything is important and urgent simultaneously.

On these mornings, I use what I call the "avalanche pause." Instead of trying to push through the overwhelm, I acknowledge it and work with it.

The Brain Dump: I spend five minutes writing down everything that's competing for my attention. Not in any particular order, not organized by priority—just getting all the mental noise out of my head and onto paper.

The Reality Check: I look at the list and ask myself: "How many of these things actually need to happen today?" Usually, the answer is much smaller than my anxious brain initially suggested.

The Single Rescue Task: From the shortened list, I choose one task that would make the biggest difference in my stress level if I completed it. This becomes my lifeline—the one thing that will help me feel more in control.

The Micro-Commitment: I commit to working on just that one task for just 10 minutes. Not to finish it, not to do it perfectly, just to make some progress and prove to myself that I can still function despite the overwhelm.

Usually, those 10 minutes are enough to break the avalanche's momentum and get me back into a more intentional rhythm.

Customizing Your Morning Reset

The specific elements of your morning reset will depend on your schedule, your living situation, and your personal preferences. The key principles are:

1. Start with internal awareness before external input. Check in with yourself before you check in with the world.

2. Choose one clear starting point rather than trying to juggle multiple priorities.

3. Create environmental conditions that support focus rather than fragment it.

4. Use time boundaries to create structure and prevent overwhelm.

5. Build in flexibility to adjust based on your energy and circumstances.

Some people prefer to do their reset ritual before getting out of bed. Others need to move their body first and then settle into the mental preparation. Some people work best with complete silence; others need background music or ambient sound.

The key is experimenting to find what works for your brain and your life, then making it consistent enough to become automatic.

> **Action Step:** Morning overwhelm isn't inevitable—it's the result of trying to process too much information before your brain is fully online.
>
> A simple reset ritual can interrupt the avalanche and set you up for an intentional day.
>
> Tomorrow morning, before you check your phone or email, spend two minutes asking

yourself: "What's one thing I could work on first that would help me feel good about how I'm starting my day?" Write it down and begin there.

Section 3:
Specialized Reset Strategies

Chapter 9: Work Reset— Deep Focus When Everything's Urgent

Everything feels urgent when you have ADHD.

The email that just arrived. The project that's due next week but feels like it should be done now. The phone call you need to make. The meeting you need to prepare for. The creative idea that just popped into your head and might disappear if you don't act on it immediately.

This false urgency is one of the most exhausting aspects of working with an ADHD brain. Your nervous system treats every task like an emergency, flooding you with stress hormones and making it nearly impossible to distinguish between what actually needs immediate attention and what just feels like it does.

I spent years bouncing between "urgent" tasks, never quite settling into the deep, focused work that actually moves important projects forward. I was constantly busy but rarely productive in the ways that mattered most.

"The enemy of deep work isn't laziness—it's the illusion that everything is equally important."

The breakthrough came when I learned to create what I call "work reset zones"—structured periods where I could step out of urgency mode and into intentional focus, even when the world around me was spinning with competing demands.

The Urgency Addiction

ADHD brains are wired to respond to urgency. We often do our best work under pressure, pull off miraculous last-minute saves, and thrive in crisis situations. This can be a genuine strength—many people with ADHD excel in emergency response, journalism, entrepreneurship, and other fields where quick thinking and rapid response are valued.

But this same urgency responsiveness becomes a trap in environments where everything is presented as urgent but very little actually is. Modern work culture, with its constant notifications, instant messaging, and "everything is a priority" mentality, exploits our urgency addiction and keeps us in a state of chronic reactivity.

I realized I had an urgency addiction when I noticed that I could only focus on tasks that felt urgent or had looming deadlines. Important but non-urgent work—strategic planning, creative projects, skill development, relationship building—consistently got pushed aside for whatever felt most pressing in the moment.

This created a cycle where I was always behind on the things that mattered most, which created real urgency, which reinforced my brain's belief that urgency was the only reliable source of motivation.

My Deep Work Disaster

The day I realized I needed a different approach was during what should have been a perfect deep work session. I had blocked off an entire afternoon for strategic planning—no meetings, no interruptions, just me and some important thinking about the direction of my business.

Within the first ten minutes, I had:

- Checked my email "just to make sure there were no emergencies."

- Found three messages that felt urgent and spent twenty minutes crafting responses.

- Received a Slack notification about a project deadline that wasn't actually urgent but triggered my anxiety.

- Started researching solutions to a problem that didn't need to be solved that day.

- Remembered a client call I needed to schedule and spent fifteen minutes playing calendar tennis.

- Got distracted by an interesting article someone had shared and spent another twenty minutes reading it.

Two hours later, I had accomplished exactly zero strategic planning and felt completely scattered and frustrated. I was exhausted from all the task-switching but had nothing meaningful to show for my effort.

That's when I realized that deep work wasn't going to happen accidentally. I needed to create systematic protection for focused work, not just hope that focus would emerge naturally.

The Anatomy of a Work Reset

A work reset isn't just about eliminating distractions—it's about creating the conditions where deep focus becomes the path of least resistance. This involves several key elements:

Environmental protection means creating physical and digital barriers that make it harder to access distractions than to stay focused. This might involve turning off notifications, using website blockers, working in a different location, or putting your phone in another room.

Cognitive preparation involves getting your brain ready for sustained attention by clarifying your intention, gathering necessary resources, and addressing any mental clutter that might interfere with focus.

Energy management means aligning your most demanding work with your natural energy rhythms and your brain's current capacity for sustained attention.

Structured flexibility creates a framework that supports focus while still allowing for the natural fluctuations in attention that come with ADHD brains.

Dominic's Deep Work Comeback

I read about Dominic, a software developer with ADHD, who struggled with deep coding sessions despite being passionate about his work.

"I loved coding, but I couldn't stay focused on complex problems for more than twenty minutes," he explained in a tech forum. "I'd get stuck on something challenging, and suddenly I'd be checking Twitter, reading documentation for a completely different project, or reorganizing my desk."

Dominic's breakthrough came when he developed what he called his "comeback loop"— a structured protocol for returning to deep work after inevitably getting distracted.

Instead of expecting himself to maintain perfect focus for hours (which never worked), he built regular distractions into his work routine. Every 25 minutes, he would allow himself a 5-minute break to do whatever his brain wanted—check notifications, stretch, or even just stare out the window.

But here's the crucial part: when the 5 minutes ended, he had a specific re-entry ritual:

1. He would state out loud: "I'm working on [specific problem]"

2. He would reread the last bit of code he wrote

3. He would write one comment about what needed to happen next

"The ritual became like a password that would unlock my focus again," Dominic shared. "I still got distracted, but I had a reliable way to come back. Eventually, the comeback loop became so automatic that I could reset my focus in seconds rather than minutes."

This approach worked because it didn't fight against Dominic's ADHD brain—it worked with it. It acknowledged that distractions would happen and built a system for returning rather than trying to eliminate distractions entirely.

My Current Work Reset Protocol

After years of experimentation, I've developed a work reset protocol that consistently helps me access deep focus even when everything around me feels urgent.

The Urgency Audit: Before I begin any focused work session, I spend two minutes identifying what feels urgent right now and asking whether it's actually urgent or just feels that way. I write down anything that's competing for my attention, not to ignore it, but to acknowledge it and consciously choose to address it later.

The Focus Commitment: I write down exactly what I'm planning to focus on and for how long. This might be "Write for 45 minutes on the client proposal introduction" or "Research for 30 minutes on the new product features." The specificity helps my brain understand what success looks like.

The Distraction Parking Lot: I keep a piece of paper next to me where I can quickly jot down anything that comes to mind during the work session. This allows me to capture important thoughts without losing focus on my primary task.

The Energy Match: I honestly assess my current energy level and choose work that matches my capacity. High-energy periods are for creative work or complex problem-solving. Medium-energy periods are for routine tasks that still require focus. Low-energy periods are for administrative work or simple completions.

The Recovery Buffer: I always plan for a few minutes of recovery time after a deep work session. This might involve walking, stretching, or just sitting quietly. It helps my brain process what I've accomplished and transition to whatever comes next.

Working with Your Ultradian Rhythms

One of the most important discoveries in my work reset journey was learning to work with my brain's natural attention cycles rather than against them.

Most people experience what researchers call "ultradian rhythms"—natural fluctuations in alertness and focus that occur throughout the day in roughly 90-minute cycles. For people with ADHD, these rhythms can be even more pronounced.

I started tracking my energy and focus levels throughout the day and noticed clear patterns. My peak focus time was usually in the morning between 9 and 11 AM. I had another good period in the early afternoon, and then my focus became much more inconsistent after about 3 PM.

Instead of fighting these rhythms, I learned to work with them. I schedule my most demanding deep work during my peak focus times. I use my medium-focus periods for routine tasks that still require attention.

During my low-focus times, I handle administrative work, take breaks, or do physical tasks that don't require sustained mental effort.

This doesn't mean being rigid about timing—some days my rhythms are different, and I adjust accordingly. But having a baseline understanding of when my brain works best has dramatically improved my ability to access deep focus when I need it.

The False Emergency Response

One of the biggest obstacles to deep work is what I call the "false emergency response"—the way our brains treat ordinary work tasks as if they were urgent crises requiring immediate attention.

An email arrives, and your brain responds as if it's a fire alarm. Someone mentions a problem in a meeting, and you feel compelled to solve it immediately. You remember a task you need to complete, and it suddenly feels like the most important thing in the world.

Learning to pause and assess whether something is actually urgent or just feels urgent has been crucial for protecting deep work time. I use what I call the "24-hour test": if this task wasn't completed in the next 24 hours, what would actually happen?

Usually, the answer is "nothing significant." This helps me distinguish between genuine urgency and the false urgency that my ADHD brain generates around most tasks.

Creating Focus Momentum

One of the most effective strategies I've discovered is starting focused work sessions with what I call "momentum builders"—small, easy tasks related to my main work that help me ease into deeper focus.

If I'm planning to write for an hour, I might start by reading and editing the last paragraph I wrote yesterday. If I'm working on a complex project, I might begin by reviewing my notes and organizing my thoughts. If I'm doing creative work, I might start with five minutes of free-form brainstorming.

These momentum builders serve several purposes:

- They help my brain transition from whatever I was doing before to focused work mode.

- They provide an easy entry point that doesn't trigger resistance or overwhelm.

- They connect me with the work I've already done, making it easier to continue.

- They often generate ideas or insights that fuel the deeper work that follows.

The key is keeping momentum builders simple and directly related to your main task. They should feel like a natural warm-up, not a separate project that could derail your focus.

When Everything Really Is Urgent

Sometimes you'll find yourself in situations where multiple truly urgent tasks are competing for your attention. In these cases, the goal isn't to eliminate urgency but to work with it more skillfully.

Triage ruthlessly: Make quick decisions about what absolutely must be done today versus what can wait until tomorrow, even if it doesn't feel good to delay things.

Batch similar urgent tasks: If you have multiple urgent emails to write, write them all in one focused session rather than spreading them throughout the day.

Use urgency as fuel: When you're genuinely working on something urgent, let that energy power your focus rather than fighting against it.

Protect recovery time: High-urgency periods are mentally and physically draining. Build in recovery time so you don't burn out.

Plan for post-crisis: Once the urgent situation is resolved, you'll likely experience an energy crash. Plan easier tasks for this period rather than expecting to maintain the same intensity.

The goal isn't to never experience urgency—it's to choose when to engage with urgency rather than being constantly reactive to it.

Action Step

Deep work requires protection from the false urgency that makes everything feel equally important.

Creating structured focus periods allows you to distinguish between what's actually urgent and what just feels that way.

Block 25 minutes on your calendar right now for focused work on one specific task.

Turn off notifications, write down your exact intention, and see what happens when you create protective boundaries around your attention.

Chapter 10: Creative Focus Reset – Finish What You Start

Creativity with ADHD is a beautiful, chaotic gift.

You're probably overflowing with ideas. You get sparks of inspiration at random hours. You're constantly starting things, sketching outlines, voice-noting concepts, or opening blank docs with enthusiasm.

But let's be real—**ADHD is great at starting. But it's terrible at finishing.**

Not because we're lazy. Because finishing is *boring*. It's tedious. It requires returning to details, making decisions, and doing things we've already lost interest in.

This chapter is about building a **Creative Focus Reset**—a set of 5-minute tools you can use to stay engaged and actually close the loop on the projects that matter.

The Creative ADHD Pattern:
Start Strong, Fade Fast

ADHD creative cycles often look like this:

1. Lightning bolt idea. You're on fire. You dive in.

2. You build momentum quickly—but don't define the finish line.

3. You hit the messy middle. Tasks pile up. It's not fun anymore.

4. A new idea shows up. It feels fresh, exciting.

5. You jump ship and start again—leaving the last project half-done.

It's not that you're flaky. It's that your brain is wired to **chase novelty**, not process.

But with the right structure, you can build momentum **and see things through.**

How I've Learned to Finish Creative Work

Early in my career, I had 10 book ideas for every one I actually finished. I'd write chapters 1-3... then start something else. Eventually, I had a digital drawer of almost-books and an overwhelming pile of "could be great" ideas.

Everything changed when I stopped trying to push through the entire project at once. Instead, I built a **micro-focus loop** for creativity:

- **Start with 5 minutes** (not "finish the chapter")

- **Work from an outline**, even if it's messy

- **Capture new ideas**, but don't switch to them

- **Define what "done for today" looks like**, before I begin

And most importantly, I made it a rule: *"I can't chase the new idea until I've closed one loop on the current one."*

It's not rigid. It's responsible creativity.

Luna's Visual Loop Lock Strategy

Luna, a graphic designer with ADHD, kept abandoning client proposals to chase new design layouts or play with new software.

"I'd get so excited about a creative direction, work on it intensely for hours, then hit a roadblock and completely lose interest," she explained. "Meanwhile, my deadlines would creep closer, and I'd end up rushing something together at the last minute."

Luna developed what she called the "Loop Lock strategy":

At the start of each session, she would write her ONE creative objective on a sticky note and place it prominently on her monitor.

She used a visual timer that showed time passing, creating a gentle sense of boundary without rigidity.

Once the objective was completed, she gave herself 10 minutes of "free explore" time to do anything creative with no rules.

"Knowing I *get* to explore later makes me want to finish the boring part first," she shared. "But the amazing thing is, once I started actually finishing things, I discovered that completion itself became rewarding."

Using this system, Luna went from completing about 30% of her projects on time to finishing over 90% of them—and the quality improved dramatically because she wasn't constantly rushing at the last minute.

Reset Tools for Creative Brains That Bounce

Here's how to build your own **Creative Focus Reset**, ADHD-style:

Step 1: Shrink the Creative Win

Forget "finish the article" or "record the episode." Try:

- Write the first 2 sentences

- Sketch 1 idea

- Name the next step in your outline

- Record the intro only

The goal is to make each creative session so small and doable that your brain can't come up with a good reason to avoid it. Then, if you want to continue after reaching that tiny goal, it's a bonus rather than an expectation.

Step 2: Anchor to Your Tools

Create rituals around your workspace:

- Use one specific chair for creative work

- Open the same music or playlist every time

- Use a physical object (pen, timer, candle) that signals: "This is my creative time"

These environmental anchors help bypass the decision fatigue that often prevents creative work from starting. When your brain associates certain objects or settings with creative flow, it becomes easier to drop into that state without overthinking.

Step 3: Define What "Done for Today" Looks Like

Before you start, answer: "What would make this session feel complete—even if the whole project isn't?"

Examples:

- "If I map the first 3 slides, I'm done."

- "If I write the episode intro, I'm done."

This stops the shame spiral of endless work and creates psychological closure. It also helps you resume more easily the next day because you know exactly where you left off and what comes next.

What to Do When a New Idea Hijacks Your Brain

New idea popping in mid-session? Try this:

1. **Capture it:** Write it in a "Later List" (keep a digital notebook, paper pad, or voice memo app)

2. **Acknowledge it:** Say, "That's a great idea. I'll come back to it."

3. **Return focus:** Go back to your micro-task

4. **Reward yourself:** Give yourself 10 minutes of free play or exploration after the loop is closed

You're not killing creativity. You're *protecting it* by ensuring that some of your ideas actually make it to completion rather than all of them staying perpetually half-finished.

My Creative Completion Ritual

I've developed a simple completion ritual for creative work that helps me push through the often tedious final stages of a project. When I'm about 80% done with something—that dangerous zone where ADHD brains are most likely to lose interest—I do the following:

I write down everything that still needs to be done to consider the project complete. Not in my task management system, but on a separate piece of paper dedicated just to this project.

I break these remaining tasks into the smallest possible components. Instead of "edit chapter 3," I'll write "fix the transition paragraph on page 24" or "check references in the section about focus."

I create artificial deadlines and rewards for these micro-completions. "After I finish reviewing these three paragraphs, I'll take a five-minute break to check social media."

The key insight that made this ritual work for me was recognizing that completion requires a completely different mindset than creation.

Once I stopped expecting the finishing work to feel as exciting as the starting work, I was able to develop different motivational strategies for each phase.

Action Step

Creative focus isn't about limiting your ideas—it's about containing your energy.

With a 5-minute reset ritual, you can build momentum, finish more, and feel proud of the work you actually complete.

Pick one creative task you've been avoiding, define "done for today" with a small, winnable goal, choose a ritual anchor (music, environment, phrase), then set a 10-15 minute timer and complete just that step.

Then stop, celebrate, and save the next step for tomorrow.

This builds your creative completion muscle one small win at a time.

Chapter 11: Design Your Daily Focus Rhythm

If mornings feel like an avalanche, evenings often feel like the leftovers.

Unfinished tasks. Open loops. Half-written emails. That "what did I even get done today?" feeling. And if you're anything like me, you've ended your day more than once sitting in front of your screen at 9:00 p.m., clicking aimlessly between tabs—not because you're working...but because your brain hasn't *logged off* yet.

I used to believe that if I could just find the perfect productivity system, all my focus problems would disappear. I tried everything: complex time-blocking, color-coded planners, habit trackers, and apps with more features than I could ever use.

Three days later, I'd abandon it all. The planners would sit untouched. The apps would send notifications I'd ignore. The schedule would crumble the first time something unexpected happened—which was basically every day.

ADHD brains don't thrive on rigid schedules—they need intentional rhythms.

Why Traditional Schedules Fail ADHD Brains

Traditional schedules require you to:

- Start tasks at specific times
- Maintain focus for predetermined durations
- Transition smoothly between activities
- Remember what comes next without prompting

These requirements directly conflict with ADHD neurological patterns, including:

- Time blindness (difficulty perceiving the passage of time)
- Variable attention spans that don't conform to preset durations
- Transition difficulties between different types of activities
- Working memory limitations that make it hard to hold schedule details

Instead of controlling time (which ADHD brains struggle with), we need to create a rhythm of intention (which plays to our strengths). This is what I call a **Focus Stack**—a series of brief, intentional reset moments that help you reconnect with your intentions throughout the day.

The Focus Stack: Reset Points Throughout Your Day

A Focus Stack is a series of intentional reset moments (2-5 minutes each) that help you:

1. Reconnect with your intentions
2. Reorient your attention
3. Choose your next move consciously

The beauty is in the simplicity and flexibility. You don't need to do your resets at exact times. You can adapt them to fit whatever is happening that day. If you miss one, you haven't "failed"—you just catch the next one.

Think of these resets as navigation checkpoints rather than rigid commitments. They create a rhythm to your day without the pressure of a schedule.

Ibrahim's Daily Rhythm Revolution

Ibrahim, a creator with ADHD, struggled with a common pattern: he couldn't mentally disconnect at night, would work until midnight, then scroll to numb the stress. He'd wake up groggy with no direction, and his days had no clear boundaries.

He developed what eventually became a complete daily rhythm with three key reset points:

Morning Launch Point (3 minutes): Write three important tasks on an index card to set clear intentions.

Midday Reset (2 minutes): After lunch, take a brief walk outside, then rewrite priorities for the rest of the day.

Evening "Tomorrow Card" Ritual (5 minutes):

1. Write down three important tasks for tomorrow
2. List any unfinished tasks from today on the back
3. Physically place the card in a box by the front door
4. Say aloud: "I'm done working for today. My brain is off duty."

"The physical act of writing down the unfinished things and literally putting them away was transformative," Ibrahim shared. "It was like telling my brain, 'You don't have to keep remembering this—it's safely captured and waiting for you tomorrow.'"

Within two weeks, he was falling asleep faster, being more present with his family, and waking up clearer. His productivity improved not because he was working more hours, but because he had created a rhythm of intention and closure.

The Unfinished Loop Problem

The ADHD brain loves to start. But it's not great at finishing—or pausing.

By the end of the day, we're often surrounded by:

- Open documents
- Vague to-dos
- Mental clutter from unclosed loops
- Guilt from what didn't get done

This makes it hard to rest... and even harder to wake up clear the next day.

The evening reset is particularly powerful because it addresses what psychologists call the "Zeigarnik effect"—your brain's tendency to keep thinking about unfinished tasks. By creating clear closure at day's end, you free up mental resources for rest and recovery.

My Current Daily Focus Stack

After years of experimentation, I've developed a simple Focus Stack that creates rhythm without rigidity:

Morning Reset (5 minutes): Before checking email or messages, I ask three questions:

- What do I want to accomplish today?
- What's my energy level right now?
- What's one specific task I could start with to build momentum?

I write down brief answers and choose one specific task to begin with. This becomes my anchor point—if I get distracted, I can return to this intention.

Midday Reset (3 minutes): When my energy naturally dips, I:

- Step away from my workspace
- Move my body briefly
- Reassess what I've accomplished and what's reasonable for the afternoon

Transition Reset (30 seconds): Before changing activities, I pause to set a clear intention for the next task.

Evening Reset (3 minutes): I write down what I accomplished, note any loose ends for tomorrow, and physically shut down my workspace. I take three deep breaths and say, "Work is done for today."

This entire system takes less than 20 minutes spread throughout my day, but creates a rhythm of returning to intention that prevents hours of distraction.

Elements of a Solid Evening Reset

Evening resets aren't about squeezing in more productivity. They're about making peace with the day.

Here's a simple formula:

1. Reflect (60-90 seconds)

- What went well today?
- What did I actually complete?
- What was the hardest moment—and how did I handle it?

This reflection counteracts the ADHD brain's tendency to focus only on what remains undone.

2. Capture Unfinished Loops (60-90 seconds)

- List 1-3 items you want to come back to
- Write them down and put them away
- Use a "Tomorrow Start" sticky note or card

Physical externalization frees up mental bandwidth and reduces anxiety.

3. Shut Down with Intention (60-90 seconds)

- Power down your work device
- Do one physical reset action: light a candle, stretch, play music, step outside
- Use a phrase like: *"Work is done. I'm off duty."*

The physical component is crucial for ADHD brains, which need concrete signals to shift between modes.

Building Your Personal Focus Stack

1. **Identify your natural patterns.** When do you typically lose focus? When does your

energy predictably dip? What transitions could serve as natural reset points?

2. **Choose 3-4 strategic reset moments:**
   - Morning transition (from sleep to work)
   - Midday energy dip (typically after lunch)
   - Task transitions (between different types of work)
   - Evening boundary (from work to rest)

3. **Create a simple reset ritual for each point** that includes:
   - Awareness (notice your current state)
   - Physical component (movement, breathing, sensory input)
   - Clear decision (what to focus on next)

4. **Keep each reset short** (2-5 minutes maximum)

5. **Practice consistency without rigidity** (times can vary, but sequence stays stable)

The Science Behind the Daily Rhythm

There's solid neuroscience behind why this approach works for ADHD brains:

Ultradian rhythms are natural 90-120 minute cycles of energy and attention that everyone experiences. For ADHD brains, these peaks and valleys can be more extreme. By creating intentional reset points that align with these natural rhythms, you're working with your brain's natural patterns rather than against them.

Task set inhibition—the ability to stop thinking about one activity when switching to another—is particularly challenging for ADHD brains. The brief reset moments create clean breaks between activities, reducing mental residue that can consume cognitive resources.

The evening reset helps shift your brain into parasympathetic (rest and digest) mode instead of staying in sympathetic (fight or flight) activation. This neurological downshift is essential for quality sleep and mental recovery.

Alternate Stack Styles

If a daily rhythm doesn't work for you, consider these alternatives:

Energy-Based Stack: Design different resets for high-energy, medium-energy, and low-energy states, using them as needed regardless of time.

Task-Type Stack: Create distinct reset rituals for transitioning between different types of work (creative, administrative, collaborative).

Location Stack: Develop reset rituals tied to physical locations or postures (desk work, meetings, deep thinking space).

The key is finding a rhythm that works with your natural patterns rather than forcing yourself into a predetermined structure.

Action Step

Your brain doesn't need a perfect schedule—it needs reliable return points and clear boundaries between work and rest. Take 10 minutes today to design your Daily Focus Rhythm:

Choose one morning reset ritual to start your day with intention rather than reaction

Identify one natural transition point in your day that could serve as a midday reset

Create a simple 3-minute evening shutdown ritual that gives your brain permission to rest

Start with just these three reset points. Once they become habitual, you can expand your

Focus Stack to include additional transition moments.

The consistency of your rhythm matters more than its complexity.

Chapter 12: Focus Reset for Overwhelm and Panic Mode

There's stuck—and then there's *spinning*.

You know the feeling:

- Your chest tightens.

- Your mind races with 10 things at once.

- You feel frozen... but also frantic.

- You can't decide what to do next—so you do nothing.

If you live with ADHD, this happens more than you'd like to admit. We don't just procrastinate. We **shut down** under pressure.

In moments like these, you don't need a to-do list. You need a nervous system reset.

Why Overwhelm Hijacks Your Brain

When overwhelm hits, your prefrontal cortex—the part of your brain that helps you make decisions and prioritize—**goes offline**.

And the ADHD brain already has a lower threshold for:

- Emotional regulation

- Uncertainty tolerance

- Cognitive overload

That means we spiral faster. And once we hit panic mode, **we can't think our way out of it.**

This is not a discipline problem. It's a **body problem**.

And that means your reset has to start *from the body up.*

My Personal "Panic Mode" Experience

There was a morning I opened my laptop and realized I had missed an important email chain. I hadn't sent a client update. My project deadline had moved. My notes were scattered. And the Dropbox folder wasn't syncing.

I felt that familiar heat behind my eyes. The thought: *"I can't do all this. I've messed it up."*

My first instinct? Fix everything right now.

But I knew better.

Instead of scrambling, I shut my laptop. I left the room. I did my **Emergency Reset**.

Five minutes later, I wasn't calm—but I was *capable.* And that made all the difference.

Arjun's Emergency Reset Walk

I read about Arjun, a software engineer with ADHD, who experienced regular midday shutdowns.

He'd be doing fine... then suddenly get three emails at once, a Slack ping, and a calendar notification. Cue overwhelm.

"It was like my brain would just freeze," he explained in an online forum. "I'd stare at my screen unable to decide what to do first, but feeling intense pressure to do everything immediately."

His response was either to freeze—or compulsively switch tasks, starting seventeen things without finishing any of them.

Arjun developed a simple three-step Emergency Reset:

1. Stand up immediately and leave his desk

2. Walk a loop around the office or block

3. Repeat the phrase "One thing, one step" while breathing

"The key was not waiting until I felt ready to move," Arjun shared. "The moment I felt that panic rising, I had to physically relocate—even if I was in the middle of something urgent."

What made this reset work wasn't the walking itself, but the interruption of the panic cycle before it could fully take hold. By changing his physical state, Arjun was able to reset his mental state as well.

"It doesn't solve everything, but it *cuts the panic cycle* before it gets out of control."

That's what we're aiming for. Not perfection—just *re-entry*.

Your Emergency Focus Reset Toolkit

Here's a simple reset you can do when overwhelm hits hard:

Step 1: Interrupt the Freeze

- Stand up

- Shake out your hands

- Walk 10 steps

- Clap, stretch, or do any quick movement

The physical interruption is crucial. ADHD brains get stuck in perseveration loops—the mental equivalent of a skipping record. Physical movement creates a pattern interrupt that can break this cycle.

Step 2: Reconnect with Your Senses

- Splash cold water on your face or hands

- Name 5 things you see, 4 you can touch, 3 you can hear

- Hold a small object and focus on the texture for 30 seconds

- Try square breathing: Inhale 4, hold 4, exhale 4, hold 4 (repeat 3x)

Sensory grounding techniques help bring your nervous system out of fight-or-flight mode by reconnecting you with the present moment. When overwhelm hits, we're often caught in anxiety about the future or regret about the past—sensory awareness anchors you in the now.

Step 3: Choose ONE Safe Action

- Write down one doable task (not urgent—just stabilizing)

- Say your focus phrase: "Back to one thing"

- Set a timer for 5-10 minutes and begin

- If that feels like too much, set it for 2 minutes. Start there.

The goal is not to finish everything. The goal is to calm the system so you can *choose again.*

Why It Works: The Science Behind the Reset

When you use your body to interrupt the panic cycle, you:

- Reduce cortisol (stress hormone)

- Signal to your brain that you're safe

- Re-engage the prefrontal cortex (decision-making center)

- Shift from threat response → intentional action

This works because of the bidirectional relationship between your body and your brain. Just as mental stress causes physical symptoms (racing heart, shallow breathing), physical interventions can create mental shifts.

The ADHD brain is particularly vulnerable to what neuroscientists call "emotional flooding"— when strong emotions overwhelm cognitive functions.

This flooding happens faster and more intensely in ADHD brains due to differences in the limbic system (emotional processing) and its connection to the prefrontal cortex (rational thinking).

By using body-based interventions, you're essentially creating a "back door" to regulate your nervous system when the front door (trying to think your way out of panic) is blocked.

Zenobia's Sensory Rescue Kit

I read about Zenobia, a teacher with ADHD, who created what she called her "Sensory Rescue Kit" after noticing that her overwhelm always followed a predictable pattern.

"I'd get a pit in my stomach, my breathing would get shallow, and I'd start feeling like everything was urgent and nothing was possible," she explained in an educational newsletter. "Once that feeling started, I had about two minutes before I'd completely shut down."

Zenobia assembled a small tin containing:

- A small bottle of essential oil (lavender for her, but any scent you find grounding works)

- A piece of very soft fabric

- A hard, textured object to hold

- A card with three written questions: "What can I see? What can I hear? What can I feel?"

She kept this tin in her desk drawer, her car, and her bag. The moment she felt overwhelm beginning, she would reach for the tin and engage with the sensory items, focusing completely on the physical sensations rather than the thoughts racing through her mind.

"The sensory focus gave my overwhelmed brain something concrete to latch onto," she shared. "It was like a reset button for my nervous system."

After using the sensory tools for 2-3 minutes, Zenobia would be calm enough to write down just one next step. Not a complete plan, not a solution to everything—just the very next action she could take.

"What I found fascinating was that the solutions that seemed impossible when I was in panic mode became obvious once my nervous system calmed down," she noted. "It wasn't that I didn't know what to do—it was that overwhelm was blocking my access to that knowledge."

Try This Now: Practice a Calm Reset (Before You Need It)

You don't have to wait for a breakdown to use this.

Take 5 minutes today:

1. Choose a movement-based interrupt (stretch, walk, shake out)

2. Choose a sensory reset (touch cold water, name 3 things you see)

3. Choose a short phrase to ground yourself ("One thing at a time")

4. Practice it now so it's ready when you need it

The key to making emergency resets work is practicing them before you need them. If you wait until you're already in full panic mode, it's much harder to remember and implement the tools.

By rehearsing your reset when you're relatively calm, you're creating neural pathways that make the reset more accessible during crisis moments. It's like practicing a fire drill—you don't wait for the building to be on fire to figure out where the exits are.

My Go-To Panic Reset

After years of experimentation, I've developed a reliable emergency reset that works even when my brain feels completely fried.

First, I step away from whatever I'm doing—physically move to a different space, even if it's just standing up from my desk and walking to the other side of the room. This physical disruption helps break the perseveration loop that often happens in ADHD overwhelm.

Next, I do what I call a "sensory sweep"—I place my hands on a cold surface (countertop, wall, window), take three deep breaths while focusing on the sensation of cold against my palms, then look around and name five things I can see in detail. This grounding technique helps bring my nervous system out of fight-or-flight mode.

Then, I write down—on paper, not digitally—exactly what I'm feeling overwhelmed about. Not solutions, just the specific concerns. "I don't know where to start on the report," or "I'm afraid I've missed something important," or "I can't decide which task to do first."

Getting these thoughts out of my head and onto paper creates psychological distance and helps my prefrontal cortex come back online.

Finally, I choose one micro-action that feels completely doable, even in my current state. Not the most important thing, not the most urgent thing—just the thing I feel capable of doing right now. Sometimes that's as simple as opening the document I need to work on, or sending one email, or organizing my desk for five minutes.

The entire reset takes less than five minutes, but it creates the conditions where I can think clearly again rather than spinning in overwhelm.

> **Action Step:** When overwhelm hits, you can't think your way to clarity. You need a body-based reset to calm the chaos and bring your brain back online.
>
> Create your Emergency Focus Reset right now: pick one movement (like standing up and stretching), one sensory anchor (like splashing cold water on your face), and choose a grounding phrase (like "one thing at a time").
>
> Practice it once today—even if you're not in overwhelm. Next time the flood hits, you won't just cope. You'll reset and re-engage.

Section 4:
Building Your
Focus System

Chapter 13: The Focus Dashboard You'll Actually Use

The notification dinged on my phone, and I felt that familiar sinking feeling in my stomach.

Another task management app reminding me that I'd set it up three weeks ago and hadn't opened it since. It was the fourth productivity system I'd abandoned that month.

My desktop was a graveyard of organizational attempts: half-configured project management tools, abandoned digital planners, note-taking apps I'd enthusiastically downloaded and promptly forgotten. Each one represented not just wasted time, but another hit to my already fragile belief that I could ever get organized.

The problem wasn't my discipline or commitment. The problem was that I was trying to use systems that fought against my brain's natural wiring instead of working with it.

Most productivity systems are designed by and for neurotypical brains. They assume you can maintain consistent attention, remember complex organizational schemes, and transition smoothly between tasks. But ADHD brains simply don't work that way.

I didn't need another comprehensive planning system. I needed something simpler, more visual, and more forgiving.

What Makes a Focus Dashboard Different?

A Focus Dashboard isn't just a simplified to-do list. It's a visual workspace designed specifically for how ADHD brains process information and make decisions.

Traditional task management systems typically suffer from several fatal flaws for people with ADHD:

- They show too much information at once, creating choice paralysis and overwhelm
- They hide completed work, robbing you of the visual evidence of progress that ADHD brains particularly need
- They require significant maintenance, creating "meta-work" that feels

productive but doesn't actually move projects forward
- They're often text-heavy and visually monotonous, failing to engage the visual processing strengths that many people with ADHD possess

A Focus Dashboard addresses these issues by creating a visual environment that externally supplements the executive function challenges that ADHD brains face internally.

My Current Dashboard Setup

I've experimented with many different formats, but what works best for me is a simple, low-tech solution that keeps important information visible without requiring complex maintenance.

My current dashboard lives on a small whiteboard next to my desk, divided into a few simple sections:

"Today's One Thing" is where I write the single most important task that would make the day feel successful if I completed nothing else. Having it identified and visible eliminates the decision fatigue that often paralyzes ADHD brains.

"Micro-Tasks" contains 3-4 small, easily completable tasks that take 5-15 minutes each. These serve as momentum builders when I'm struggling to focus on larger projects.

"In Progress Projects" shows the 1-2 active projects I'm currently focusing on, with the specific next action step for each one clearly identified. Limiting this section to just 1-2 active projects forces me to make conscious decisions about what deserves my attention right now.

"Avoid List" might seem unusual, but it's where I list activities that often masquerade as work but are actually forms of productive procrastination: reorganizing my file system, researching new productivity tools, or spending too long perfecting unimportant details.

Finally, I include a simple **"Mood/Focus Tracker"**—just a word or color that represents how I'm feeling. This helps me match my tasks to my current mental state instead of fighting against it.

The entire dashboard takes less than two minutes to update each morning, and it gives me a clear focal point throughout the day.

Esmeralda's Kitchen Table Dashboard

Esmeralda, a content creator with two young children, was feeling completely overwhelmed by her work. She had clients waiting for deliverables, half-finished projects scattered across her laptop, and constant interruptions from her kids.

Without a dedicated office space, she created a simple paper dashboard in a plastic sleeve taped to the wall next to her regular seat at the kitchen table. Her dashboard included:

A clear **"One Thing"** section for the single most important task for that work session, regardless of duration.

A **"Tiny Tasks"** section with 2-3 small actions she could complete during micro-sessions—perfect for those brief windows when both kids were momentarily occupied.

A visual **"In Progress"** section to see what client work was actively moving forward.

A **"Done This Week"** area where she tracked completed work, creating a visible record of progress.

The physical placement was crucial—it was the first thing she saw when she sat down at her workspace, requiring no additional steps to access.

"This lets me work like a real human again," she shared. "I don't need to feel guilty about everything else—I just focus on what's here. And when I'm interrupted, I don't come back and waste twenty minutes trying to remember what I was doing."

Finding Your Dashboard Format

The right Focus Dashboard format depends on your specific needs, preferences, and work environment. The key is finding an approach that gives you clarity without creating maintenance overhead.

For physical thinkers and visual learners, a paper-based dashboard often works best. This can be as simple as a single sheet of paper divided into 3-4 sections. The tactile experience of writing by hand can help reinforce priorities and create stronger memory traces than digital input.

If you need physical engagement and novelty, a sticky note dashboard might be ideal. Different colored notes can represent different types of tasks, and the physical act of moving notes provides tangible feedback and satisfaction.

For those who primarily work digitally, a simple digital dashboard can work well—but simplicity is key. A single note in your preferred app, a basic Notion page, or a minimalist Trello board can serve the same function without overwhelming complexity.

Whichever format you choose, the core principles remain the same: keep it visual, limit the information to what's truly important right now, make it easy to update, and ensure it's always visible while you're working.

Building Your First Dashboard

Creating your first Focus Dashboard doesn't need to be complicated or time-consuming. The simpler you make it, the more likely you are to actually use it consistently.

Start with the four core sections that most ADHD brains need for clarity:

- **"Today's One Thing"** - The single most important task that would make today feel successful

- **"Micro-Tasks"** - Two to four small, easily completable tasks that can build momentum
- **"In Progress"** - One or two active projects with their specific next steps clearly identified
- **"Avoid List"** - Activities that feel productive but are actually forms of procrastination

You can add other elements that might be helpful for your specific situation, but resist the temptation to overcomplicate. The power of the dashboard is in its focused simplicity.

The most important consideration is visibility. Your dashboard should be immediately accessible whenever you're working, without requiring you to open an app, flip to a specific page, or remember to check it.

Update your dashboard at the beginning of each day or work session, but keep this process quick and simple. It should take no more than 2-3 minutes.

The Power of Visual Focus

The reason Focus Dashboards work so well for ADHD brains comes down to how we process information and make decisions. ADHD creates challenges with working memory, prioritization, and initiation.

A well-designed dashboard externally supplements these internal executive function challenges:

- It holds important information visually so you don't have to keep it in working memory
- It makes priorities explicit so you don't have to repeatedly decide what matters most
- It reduces startup friction by clearly identifying next actions

This external scaffolding doesn't cure ADHD, but it creates conditions where your natural strengths can shine without being undermined by executive function challenges. It's like wearing glasses if you have vision problems—the glasses don't change your eyes, but they create an environment where you can see clearly despite your visual challenges.

When you have a system that actually works for your brain, you stop internalizing organizational struggles as character flaws. You realize that your previous difficulties weren't due to laziness or incompetence—they were the result of trying to use systems fundamentally mismatched to how your brain processes information.

Action Step: Your brain doesn't need a complex productivity system—it needs clear visual guidance about what matters right now.

Take five minutes to create a minimalist Focus Dashboard: grab a sheet of paper or open a new digital note, divide it into four quadrants (One Thing, Micro-Tasks, In Progress, Avoid List), fill in just those sections for today, and place it where you'll see it throughout your work session.

Notice how this affects your clarity and focus compared to your traditional to-do list or task management system.

Chapter 14: When You Fall Off – Reset Fast and Build a Focus-First Identity

Let's be honest: You're going to fall off.

You're going to forget the reset.

You'll scroll when you meant to focus.

You'll miss a day. Maybe a few.

And that's okay.

Falling off isn't the problem. Spiraling is.

ADHD brains are sensitive to failure. We internalize mistakes.

We tell ourselves stories like:

- "I'll never get this right."
- "Why can't I just follow through?"
- "All that progress is gone."

But here's the truth:

Nothing is ruined.

Focus isn't a streak. It's a skill.

And every moment is a chance to reset.

The Shame Spiral Trap

Here's what a typical spiral looks like for an ADHD brain:

1. You skip one reset.
2. You feel behind.
3. You start avoiding your tools.
4. You convince yourself you've "lost momentum."
5. You abandon the system completely.
6. Weeks later, you start over from scratch—burned out and ashamed.

Sound familiar?

The spiral doesn't start because you failed. It starts because you **judged** the fall.

And that's the real reset we need to learn.

My Reset Recovery Moment

There was a week where everything broke down.

I got sick. My routine fell apart. I stopped doing morning resets, skipped my dashboard updates, and abandoned my 5-minute rituals.

I spiraled.

But one day, I wrote a sticky note and put it next to my laptop:

"Just one reset today."

That note saved me.

Not because I suddenly became productive again. But because I gave myself **permission to begin again without punishment.**

Tori's 3-Word Recovery Rule

Tori is an ADHD educator who built a daily reset habit... and then lost it completely during a busy launch.

She ghosted her dashboard, stopped journaling, and felt like she had "failed the system."

We gave her a single rule:

Whenever she noticed the spiral, she'd say out loud: "Reset, not restart."

Then she'd do **just one reset**—even if it was 60 seconds.

Over time, her shame cycles got shorter. Her recovery time got faster.

That's what success actually looks like.

What to Do When You've Fallen Off

Step 1: Say This to Yourself

"This is a normal part of the process. I'm not behind. I just need one reset."

Step 2: Pick the Easiest Possible Action

- Open your focus dashboard
- Do a 2-minute micro-task
- Do a 3-breath reset
- Write down one task
- Close all tabs and choose one window

This isn't about rebuilding everything. It's about interrupting the spiral with a small win.

Step 3: Resume Without Guilt

You don't need to apologize to your journal. You don't need to make up for lost time. You just continue.

Why Identity Matters More Than Discipline

Willpower is unreliable. It's strongest when things are easy—and weakest when you need it most.

But identity? That's powerful.

Because once you start seeing yourself as someone who:

- Resets fast
- Reclaims attention
- Chooses the next micro-action
- Returns without shame

...you *act accordingly.*

Behavior follows belief.

And belief is shaped by **what you do repeatedly.**

When you do something because it's part of who you are, it requires far less mental effort than doing something because you're forcing yourself to. Identity-based actions feel intrinsically motivated rather than externally imposed.

Think about something deeply connected to your sense of self. Maybe you're "a person who keeps promises" or "someone who is kind to animals." You don't need willpower to act in accordance with these identities—acting against them would feel deeply uncomfortable.

What if focusing felt like an expression of your authentic self rather than a battle against your natural tendencies?

The ADHD Identity Trap

Many of us grow up believing:

- "I'm just bad at focus."
- "I never finish things."
- "I'll always be scattered."
- "I can't be trusted with structure."
- "Planning doesn't work for me."

These thoughts become *stories*.

And those stories become *identity statements*.

The problem with these identity statements isn't just that they feel bad—it's that they create a self-fulfilling prophecy. When you believe you're inherently incapable of sustained attention, you're less likely to attempt tasks that require it.

When you inevitably struggle (as all humans do, ADHD or not), you interpret it as evidence that you were right about yourself all along.

This creates a negative feedback loop where your beliefs shape your actions, your actions produce results that confirm your beliefs, and those reinforced beliefs drive future actions in the same direction.

But those identities were shaped by systems that didn't work for your brain. They were based on external expectations, not internal truth.

You get to change the story now. Not by pretending.

But by **proving to yourself who you are— through action.**

How I Rewrote My Identity—
One Reset at a Time

For years, I told myself: "I'm great at starting, terrible at finishing."

I had the evidence: abandoned drafts, missed deadlines, scattered focus.

But something changed when I started building small focus wins into my day. Just a 5-minute reset here. One task done there. One evening shutdown. One page written.

It was slow. But steady.

Instead of saying "I'm bad at focus," I started saying "I'm working on my focus skills." Instead of "I never finish projects," I tried "I'm learning to close loops more consistently." Instead of "I'm always distracted," I shifted to "I notice when my attention drifts."

These weren't just semantic games. They created space between my core self and my executive function challenges—to see these challenges as things I experienced rather than who I was.

Each time I successfully caught myself drifting and gently redirected my attention, I was casting a vote for my new identity as "someone who notices when they're distracted and knows how to come back."

Every small win became evidence of who I was becoming, not just what I was achieving.

How to Step into Your Focus-First Identity

Here's how to reinforce your new identity—without forcing it:

1. Use Identity Language

Instead of "I'm trying to focus," say:

- "I'm becoming someone who resets fast."
- "I'm someone who finishes small things on purpose."
- "I build clarity into my day—even in chaos."

Say it aloud. Write it down. Believe it over time.

2. Track Wins, Not Just Tasks

Focus on identity-building moments:

- You noticed the drift
- You did one reset
- You avoided a spiral
- You completed a micro-action
- You started again after falling off

Those aren't productivity stats.

They're **proof** of your transformation.

3. Reflect Often

Ask yourself weekly:

- What did I do this week that proves I'm someone who can focus again?
- What reset made me feel most like myself?
- Where did I return—even when I could've avoided?

That's how you lock in the change.

The power of identity-based change isn't just psychological—it's neurological. Your brain physically changes based on the stories you tell yourself and the behaviors you repeatedly practice.

When you consistently think of yourself as "scattered" or "unfocused," you strengthen neural pathways associated with those beliefs. Your reticular activating system becomes primed to notice evidence that confirms this identity while overlooking contradictory information.

Conversely, when you begin to see yourself as someone who can direct attention intentionally (even if imperfectly), you start to create new neural pathways. Each successful focus moment physically rewires your brain.

What's particularly powerful about identity-based change for people with ADHD is that it works with the brain's reward system rather than against it. ADHD brains are highly responsive to immediate rewards and positive feedback.

Action Step: Create Your Reset Recovery Plan

Complete this sentence:

"I'm someone who _____, even when _____."

Examples:

"I'm someone who comes back to focus, even when I feel behind."

"I'm someone who resets quickly, even when my brain wants to scroll."

"I'm someone who builds structure in ways that work for my ADHD brain."

Write this statement somewhere visible and say "Reset, not restart" whenever you notice yourself falling into old patterns. Then choose one micro-action to prove your new identity true.

Remember: Falling off is part of the process. The difference between spiraling and succeeding is how quickly you return—and how you're building your identity with each small reset.

Conclusion: One Reset at a Time

You've made it to the end—but this isn't really the end.

It's your next beginning.

Because the truth is, focus isn't something you arrive at once and for all. It's something you *return to*. Again and again.

And now you know how.

Moving Forward: Your Implementation Plan

Rather than trying to implement every technique at once (which would ironically create the overwhelm we're trying to solve), I recommend a graduated approach that builds sustainable change:

Week 1: Start with Awareness

Choose one drift detection technique from Chapter 3 and practice it daily:

- The 10-minute check-in timer
- The breath anchor
- The physical reset
- The curiosity question

Don't worry about "fixing" your focus yet—just notice your patterns. Where does your attention go? When do you typically drift? What triggers your loops?

This awareness alone will begin to change your relationship with focus.

Week 2: Add One Reset Ritual

Once you've built some awareness, add a single reset ritual that addresses your most pressing focus challenge:

- If mornings are your struggle, implement the Morning Reset from Chapter 9
- If overwhelm is your primary issue, practice the Emergency Reset from Chapter 13
- If environment is your biggest challenge, apply the Space Reset from Chapter 7
- If finishing things is your weakness, try the Loop Closure technique from Chapter 8

Choose just ONE reset and practice it consistently for a week before adding anything else.

Week 3: Build Your Focus Stack

Now that you've established one solid reset practice, begin developing your Daily Focus Stack from Chapter 12:

1. Identify 3-4 natural transition points in your day
2. Create a simple 2-3 minute reset ritual for each transition
3. Use these resets to reconnect with your intentions throughout the day

Remember, consistency matters more than perfection. It's better to do a simple reset consistently than a complex one occasionally.

Week 4: Develop Your Recovery Protocol

This is when you prepare for the inevitable lapses that will occur:

1. Create your personal reset phrase ("Reset, not restart")
2. Identify your smallest possible re-entry action

3. Practice your recovery process before you need it

This preparation ensures that when you fall off track (and you will), you'll have a clear path back.

When You'll Need Different Resets

Different situations call for different techniques. Here's your quick reference guide:

When you're scattered and can't start: Use the Morning Reset (Ch. 9) or the Micro-Action technique (Ch. 6)

When everything feels urgent: Apply the Work Reset (Ch. 10) to distinguish between true and false urgency

When you're overwhelmed to the point of panic: Implement the Emergency Reset (Ch. 13) to calm your nervous system first

When you can't finish what you start: Use the Creative Focus Reset (Ch. 11) and Loop Closure (Ch. 8)

When you keep getting interrupted: Apply the Environment Reset (Ch. 7) and One-Tab Rule (Ch. 2)

When you're exhausted at day's end: Practice the Evening Reset ritual (Ch. 12) to create psychological closure

When you've fallen off completely: Use your Recovery Protocol (Ch. 16) to return without shame

---

Remember Your Why

As you implement these techniques, keep sight of why you're doing this.

It's not about becoming superhuman or matching some neurotypical standard of productivity.

It's about reclaiming your agency. It's about finishing the things that matter to you. It's about being present in your own life.

Focus isn't valuable because it makes you more productive. Focus is valuable because it allows you to direct your extraordinary ADHD brain toward the things you care about, rather than being pulled in a thousand different directions.

Your Final Reset

Before we part ways, I invite you to do one more reset:

Take a deep breath. Feel your feet on the ground. Notice where your attention is right now.

Ask yourself: What's one small focus win I want to create today?

It might be a 5-minute work session on a project you've been avoiding. It might be closing unnecessary browser tabs. It might be doing a proper evening shutdown before bed.

Whatever it is, make it small enough that your brain can't find a good reason to resist it.

Then do just that one thing.

Because that's how focus works with an ADHD brain. Not through grand transformations or perfect systems, but through small, intentional resets that gradually reshape how you engage with the world.

You don't need to become someone different. You just need to keep returning to who you already are— someone capable of directing your attention, one reset at a time.

That's not just a strategy. That's freedom.

And it starts right now, with your very next choice.

"You're not starting from scratch. You're starting from experience—with a reset in your pocket and the proof that you can begin again, every time you need to."

"The more focused you are, the more successful you will be."

– Tony Robbins

BONUS CHAPTER: The ADHD Money Collision [From the 5-Minute Money Reset]

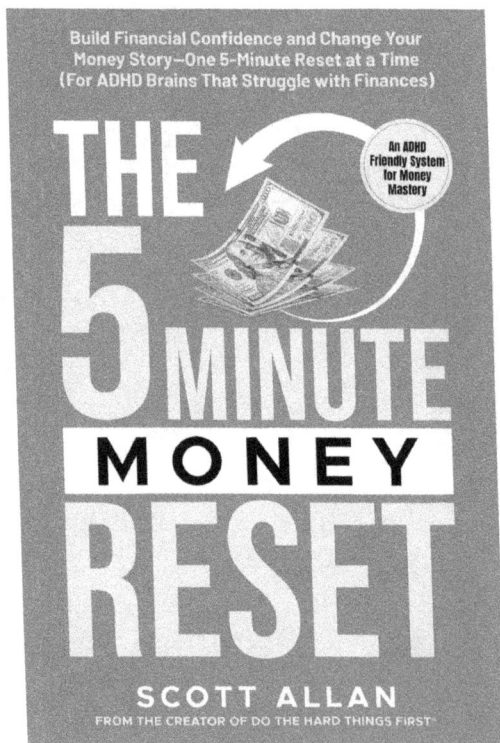

Chapter 1: The ADHD-Money Collision

Why Smart People Still Struggle with Their Finances

You can be brilliant, creative, hardworking—and still feel like your finances are a disaster.

This isn't because you're lazy. Or because you "just need a budget." It's because **ADHD and money collide in invisible, exhausting ways.**

What Nobody Told You About ADHD and Finances

If you live with ADHD, managing money doesn't just feel hard. It feels overwhelming, emotional, and sometimes impossible.

You might recognize these patterns:

- You avoid looking at accounts until something bounces

- You overspend impulsively, then feel deep regret

- You miss bills or due dates, even when you have the money

- You start tracking expenses—then abandon it after two days

- You feel like you can't trust yourself with money

These aren't character flaws. They're **functional symptoms** of how your brain processes time, emotion, and executive tasks.

The ADHD-Money Loop

Here's what typically happens:

1. You make a financial mistake (late bill, overdraft, big purchase)

2. You feel shame or panic

3. You avoid checking accounts because it's "too much"

4. Avoidance creates more chaos

5. The chaos confirms your belief: *"I'm bad with money"*

This loop reinforces **financial learned helplessness**—where you stop trying because every attempt seems doomed.

But here's the truth: You're not failing because you can't manage money. You're struggling because traditional money management **wasn't built for your brain.**

Why Typical Financial Advice Doesn't Work

Most personal finance systems assume you can:

- Track everything daily

- Plan months ahead

- Delay gratification without stress

- Stay consistent under pressure

- Manage small tasks without forgetting

ADHD disrupts all of that. We deal with:

- **Time blindness** (due dates sneak up or disappear)

- **Working memory gaps** (systems don't "stick")

- **Task initiation issues** (even small actions feel heavy)

- **Emotional reactivity** (money triggers shut us down)

- **Shame loops** (believing we "should be better" by now)

My Breaking Point

I remember sitting at my kitchen table, staring at my phone. I had my banking app open but couldn't bring myself to tap it.

The balance wasn't even the issue. It was the **feeling**—the tension in my chest, the shame in my gut, the voice whispering, *"If you were responsible, you wouldn't be here again."*

I wasn't broke. I wasn't reckless. But I was **disconnected**—from my money, my numbers, and myself.

So I did something strange. I didn't close the app. I didn't try to fix anything. I just kept it open and took a breath.

That was my first money reset. And it changed everything.

Real Story: Tara's Avoidance Spiral

Tara is a 35-year-old freelance web designer with ADHD. She makes decent money—but she never seems to know where it goes. She avoids her bank account, leaves invoices untracked, and defaults to credit cards during every crisis.

Every few months, she tells herself she'll "get it together." She downloads a budgeting app, tries for a few days, gets overwhelmed, and quits.

Eventually she stopped trying altogether—until a bounced rent payment forced her to look. Her anxiety was through the roof.

We didn't start with budgeting. We started with one simple reset: **Open the account. Breathe. That's enough for today.**

That reset was the doorway to a full transformation. But it had to start with safety—not shame.

What This Book Offers

This is not a budgeting manual. It's a **reset manual**—built specifically for ADHD brains that feel stuck, overwhelmed, or ashamed.

Every chapter gives you:

- **One five-minute action** to rebuild clarity or control

- **Realistic examples** of how ADHD brains can succeed without pressure

- **Zero shame-based language**

- **Clear prompts and checklists**

- **Repeatable systems** that build momentum without burnout

You don't need to overhaul your finances. You just need a path back into the game—one small reset at a time.

What You'll Learn in the Chapters Ahead

In this book, you'll learn how to:

- Open avoided accounts without panic

- Cancel money leaks and get your power back

- Track small wins instead of overwhelming spreadsheets

- Build reward budgets that keep you on track

- Create systems that work when your motivation doesn't

- Redefine your earning identity and rebuild financial trust

- Reset after financial mess-ups without spiraling into shame

- Navigate crises and difficult conversations with confidence

- Build support systems that sustain your progress

This is not a magic cure. It's a **daily micro-reset system** that gently rewires how you approach your money.

And it works. Not because it's hard. But because it's *built for the way you work.*

Key Takeaway

You're not bad with money. You've just never had a system that meets your brain where it is.

What to Do Next

Start where you are. The first reset isn't about fixing anything. It's about **noticing** where you've shut down—and choosing to re-engage, gently.

You're not broken. You just need a different approach. Let's take the next step together—one small reset at a time.

About Scott Allan

SCOTT ALLAN is an international bestselling author of 40+ books published in 16 languages in the area of personal growth and self-development. He is the author of *Fail Big*, *Undefeated*, and *Do the Hard Things First*.

As a former corporate business trainer in Japan, and **Transformational Mindset Strategist**, Scott has invested over 10,000 hours of research and instructional coaching into the areas of self-mastery and leadership training.

With an unrelenting passion for teaching, building critical life skills, and inspiring people around the world to take charge of their lives, Scott Allan is committed to a path of **constant and never-ending self-improvement**.

You can connect with Scott at:

- www.scottallanbooks.com

- Join Scott Allan's Newsletter

Also Available in the Series

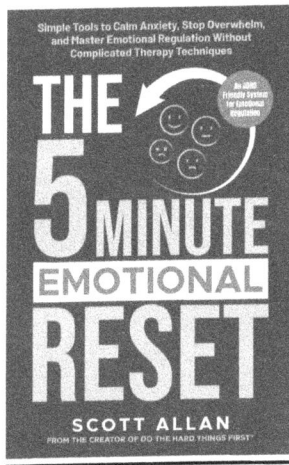

Join the 30 Day Do the Hard Things First Challenge [Course]

Join Today by clicking here or scanning the QR Code:

Use the promo code **sco28** and lock in your 30% discount

www.ingramcontent.com/pod-product-compliance
Lightning Source LLC
Chambersburg PA
CBHW022050020426
42335CB00012B/628